AFLOAT

GUY DE MAUPASSANT

Afloat

Translated from the French and with an Introduction by
MARLO JOHNSTON

With a selection of drawings by
E. RIOU

PETER OWEN
London & Chester Springs

PETER OWEN PUBLISHERS
73 Kenway Road London SW5 0RE
Peter Owen books are distributed in the USA by
Dufour Editions Inc. Chester Springs PA 19425–0007

Translated from the French *Sur l'eau*
First published in Great Britain 1889
This edition first published 1995
English translation © Marlo Johnston 1995

Drawings by E. Riou from the original French edition
published by C. Marpon et E. Flammarion, Paris, 1888

ISBN 0–7206–0966–6

A catalogue record for this book is available
from the British Library

Printed and made in Great Britain by
Biddles of Guildford and King's Lynn

CONTENTS

Introduction   7

Acknowledgements   15

Maps

The Côte d'Azur as Maupassant knew it   16

Cannes to Antibes   17

Saint-Raphaël to Saint-Tropez   18

AFLOAT   19

Appendices   115

War   117

In the Presence of Death   124

The Carthusian Monastery of La Verne   129

Chronology   137

Select Bibliography   143

INTRODUCTION

Afloat (*Sur l'eau*) was first published as a book in June 1888 (Marpon et Flammarion, illustrated with drawings by E. Riou), but it had already been serialized in three issues of the lavish magazine *Les Lettres et les arts* in February, March and April of the same year. As well as an astonishing number of short stories and newspaper articles, Maupassant had already published four of the six novels he was to write: *Une vie*, *Bel-Ami*, *Mont-Oriol* and *Pierre et Jean*. So when he was preparing *Afloat*, he was very successful, a writer in full command of his literary powers. Though he wrote two other travel books, *Au soleil* and *La Vie errante*, *Afloat* is not quite like them or any of his other books.

The first English translation was published in February 1889 (*Afloat*, Routledge, translated by Laura Ensor). At the time, very little Maupassant was available in English, and not a single one of his short stories, though many had been translated into other languages long before. Indeed, even today only three of Maupassant's six novels and only a selection of his short stories are in print in English, and there is some material that has never been translated. Henry Vizetelly was, in 1887, the first to publish Maupassant in English; *A Woman's Life* (*Une vie*) and *A Ladies' Man* (*Bel-Ami*) were both appallingly (and anonymously!) translated, as well as drastically cut for the taste of the prudish and hypocritical

7

English. Bowdlerized though the books were, Vizetelly was prosecuted and imprisoned for the publication of those and several other books. The modest success of *Afloat* was probably due to its not needing heroic expurgation, and to its acceptable and varied subject matter.

Things had improved by the 1920s, when what was intended to be a Complete Works (Werner Laurie, translated by Marjorie Laurie) began to appear. It was not complete, but it did include *Afloat*. Though the translations were much better, there were significant omissions or attenuations where Maupassant's directness (for he was not at all obscene) went beyond what the period could tolerate. Some of his admirers in England – among them Henry James, Joseph Conrad, Ford Madox Ford, Cunninghame Graham, John Galsworthy, Somerset Maugham – had read Maupassant in the original French. They knew that he had not been well translated, and four of them provided introductions to new translations.

Though Ford Madox Ford and Cunninghame Graham discussed the difficulties in their introductions, the idea that translating Maupassant is easy persisted:

> [Y]ou begin to wonder if it isn't precisely the nullity of Maupassant, the common banality of his thought, the dreary platitude of his analyses, the mediocre indigence of his style which have eased his credit beyond our borders. It goes without saying that his work is more accessible to a foreigner than the work of Rabelais, Racine or Proust can be, being the easier to translate as his language is the poorer and his psychology more limited. (Raymond Guérin, *La Parisienne*, January 1954, my translation)

That negative view of Maupassant, typical of the years leading up to the 1950s, has changed. Critical opinion in France has altered beyond recognition between the centenary of his birth, in 1950, and that of his death, in 1993, and he is now acknowledged to be a great writer.

The greatest difficulty with translating Maupassant – the extremely concise clarity, the deceptive simplicity of his language – at the same time provides the greatest pleasure. Each word is carefully chosen and no word is redundant – 'every epithet a paying piece', as Henry James put it. Finding the only one that will do is a challenge, and surprisingly often a very literal translation is the only answer. It is difficult, too, to keep the brevity, the form, the rhythm, as so often the English is longer. But these are all part of what Maupassant called the almost invisible thread, which the translator must see and respect. And all of this makes it particularly important that there should be a new English translation of *Afloat*, which has been out of print in English for so long. It is an essential book for understanding Maupassant and seems to be more intentionally personal than his other work.

However, *Afloat* was not written quite as its author would have us believe, that is, as a journal written on board his boat on consecutive days of a specific cruise. Maupassant had gone on not one, but three short cruises along the Mediterranean coast the previous spring. He wrote to his cousin on 6 March 1887 from Saint-Tropez: 'We went through a terrible storm which took my dinghy away and threw it on the coast in a thousand pieces – but the *Bel-Ami* is fearless and she came into port safe and sound.' In *Afloat* this storm occurs on the return to Antibes. There were many other short cruises, such as the one in the spring of 1886 before he had the *Bel-Ami*, when he wrote to his friend Madame Lecomte du Noüy saying he was sailing and writing. This letter contains a long passage on royalty at Cannes and also expresses the idea that if one hopes to keep integrity of thought, then social relations are to be avoided; both views were later developed in *Afloat*.

Gérard Delaisement demonstrated long ago that Maupassant in fact brought together, under the umbrella of a daily diary, parts of more than thirty newspaper articles and stories. Some of the extracts he used in *Afloat* were long, some extremely short; some were almost contemporary, while others were from several years back. The earliest is 'La Guerre' ('War'). Maupassant first wrote an article with this title in early 1881, then again in late 1883; both were a response to current political situations. It is perfectly clear that Maupassant felt a personal hatred of war, and there were very good reasons for it, since he had been in the Franco-Prussian War at the age of twenty. Most unusually, there was a witness to his feelings at the time *Afloat* was published, who noted that Maupassant, normally reticent on the subject matter of his books, made an exception for Count von Moltke and was quite beside himself, or at least to the extent that such a calm and sceptical person could be.

Unhappy personal experience undoubtedly lies behind many of the passages he reused, like that on the miserable lives of government employees. Maupassant had worked in two Ministries over eight years, and his long period in the Marine Ministry, in particular, was not forgotten. The account of his migraine and the use of ether to treat it are also certainly drawn from life and are amply documented. To contrast with the unhappy moments, there is humour and a touch of wicked delight in his observation of the society women with collections of musicians and writers; he was one of the collected writers. He had no illusions about it and the irony is clear.

Personal opinion accounts for the extracts used from another dozen articles – on conversation, both banal and witty, about the ugliness of people and his dislike of crowds (also noted by someone who knew him). All the poets quoted in *Afloat* had been mentioned in earlier articles, especially Louis Bouilhet. Many stories use moonlight and its effects and Maupassant seems to have been very responsive to that particular form of beauty. His knowledge of other writers, notably Flaubert, is revealed in his comments on how writers differ from other men, as is obvious self-analysis.

Some pieces are less obviously personal, such as the story of Bazaine's escape. The original article (1883) shows that Maupassant visited the prison and heard the details just before writing it. Bazaine was very much in the news; a book with his own story had recently come out, and the governor of the prison had also just published his version of the escape, and Maupassant added a previously unknown account he had just heard. Many of his articles came about like this, as a response to what was news. The lyrical passage on his dream of the Orient first appeared in an article, 'L'Orient' (1883), and told of a friend who lived on the frontiers of Asia. It is unclear whether the friend was real or imagined, and whether the ideas he expressed were Maupassant's, but Maupassant had spent some months in Algeria in 1881 and he used his experiences there in his writing. His love for North Africa was genuine enough. It is likely that the account of the mother and child with diphtheria was something he had seen for himself, since he went to his house at Etretat in Normandy every autumn for the start of the hunting season.

Maupassant's intention was to keep himself out of his fiction, at least in easily identifiable form, but he frequently revealed himself in his articles, and he reused more parts of articles than short stories in *Afloat*. He wrote regular columns in two newspapers, and in journalism of that kind, the character and personal quirks of the journalist are necessary and desirable, especially as in Maupassant's day the quality of the articles, short stories and serialized fiction was often what made people buy the paper. He intentionally presented a personal point of view and prided himself on his acknowledged impartiality; it was, so to speak, one of his selling points.

The real and the imaginary are difficult to separate in the account of the colonel's daughter who eloped with the hussar. There were two earlier versions: a short story and an article, both from 1884. The story, 'Happiness' ('Le Bonheur'), transferred the couple to Corsica, and emphasized the nature of love; there is no unhappy ending. 'Short Journeys: The Carthusian Monastery of La Verne' ('Petits voyages: La Chartreuse de la Verne') appeared a few months after the story. It mentions many places later featured in *Afloat*: the Maures mountains, the Argens river, new resorts, Moorish houses and the Carthusian monastery. But the account of the monastery has none of the overwhelming sadness that pervades the passage in *Afloat*, only the beauty of the view. The old couple do appear in the article, which contains only the kernel of their love story.

'Log Book' ('Livre de bord') appeared in August 1887, soon after Maupassant's cruise in the spring and about six months before *Afloat*. There is a narrator, and the boat, *The Mandarin*, belongs to his friend, while an extract from the friend's log book provides the form. The lovers at Agay feature, and the mixture of thoughts, events and nautical details seems like a preliminary sketch for *Afloat*.

The idea for 'Log Book' itself may well have come from 'Fishing-Ports and Warrior-Towns' ('Pêcheuses et guerrières', March 1887), published first as an article and later as a preface to *La Grande Bleue*, a book about the sea by Maupassant's friend René Maizeroy. Maupassant was asked to write the preface just before he set out in his yacht in the spring of 1887, and he suggests in it that his friend should write a book about a cruise round all the small, unspoiled fishing-ports on the coast of France. Maupassant wrote that he only knew two such in the Midi, Antibes and Saint-Tropez, and he reused some short passages from the article. *Afloat* could have begun with that idea, and led to the writing of some kind of journal on the cruise.

It seems legitimate to ask at this point if the book is anything more than a skilful assembly of materials to hand. Maupassant was well used to recycling what he wrote and making it produce income several times over in different publications: he was his own highly successful agent. However, most of the book is not recycled but original. The previously published material amounts to a little over a third,* but it was not simply a matter of cut and paste. At times, entire sections were taken *en bloc* (like that of the mother and child with diphtheria); sometimes only the general idea with a phrase or two; sometimes so little that the word 're-use' is scarcely appropriate; and sometimes quite a long section was used but edited (occasionally heavily, like that on the Kings of France). The majority have been reworked and interspersed with original material in such a way that the work involved was considerable, sometimes more than starting from scratch. There are also instances where some passages used appear to be almost identical, but the mood or conclusion is subtly different in *Afloat*. 'In the Presence of Death' ('Chez la mort') is one example. Though the subject is essentially the same in article and book, the book leaves quite a different impression.[†]

The fascination of the hunt to discover how Maupassant came to create *Afloat* can be distracting, but it shows that by far the greater part of the book had not previously appeared in any other form. In particular, the passages about sailing, the *Bel-Ami*, Bernard, Raymond, the sea and the wind, are all original. This is the first time Maupassant gave free rein to his thoughts on sailing, and these form some of the most beautiful parts of *Afloat*, personal and intensely felt. Maupassant's writing about water – sea, river or marsh – is indisputably a reflection of his intuitive feelings about it; its beauty and its sensuality moved him.

---

* It is difficult to be accurate as there are three sources: the Juin edition of the *Chroniques* (1980), the Pléiade edition of the *Contes et nouvelles* (1974, 1979) and microfilms of the original newspapers for those not published, as well as the Folio edition of *Sur l'eau* (1993) – all of differing formats.

[†] The reader interested in Maupassant's varying treatment of similar subjects will find translations of three articles in the Appendix: 'War' ('La Guerre', 1881), 'Short Journeys' ('Petits voyages: La Chartreuse de la Verne'), 'In the Presence of Death' ('Chez la mort'). None of them has been previously translated into English, and the last one has not been published in France since its original appearance in 1882.

His passion for boats and sailing started in his childhood in Normandy. One of the earliest known descriptions of him, by Flaubert's niece (he was probably about eight years old), sets him in the garden of his grandmother's house at Fécamp, within sight of the sea, blown by the sea breezes and near the smell of salting herrings: 'A bank of grass at the foot of a group of trees played an important part in our games. Guy had turned it into a ship. . . . [He] acted as captain and though I was four years older than he was, I was always under his command. The words port and starboard were constantly on the lips of my little friend. . . . His relish for everything involving the sea was already obvious.'

By the time Maupassant was fourteen he was saving up for a boat and during his life he came to own, or part-own, a good number – rowing boats, sailing dinghies, big yachts – he always had a boat of some sort, and often several. In his twenties, in Paris, with little money and access to the sea less easy, he had a passion for rowing on the Seine, returning to Normandy and the sea only for holidays. As he earned more from writing, in his thirties, he began to spend time in the South of France, and he bought the *Louisette*, followed a few years later by the *Bel-Ami*. This yacht, the *Bel-Ami* of *Afloat*, was named after the book *Bel-Ami* (1885). Maupassant bought her at Antibes, and here too began his important relationship with his crew, the two sailors Bernard and Raymond. *Bel-Ami* was an 11-metre cutter (formerly the *Flamberge*, first owned by the writer Paul Saunière) built in 1881 by Texier, a highly respected boatbuilder probably known to Maupassant since his yard was not far from Argenteuil on the Seine, the scene of many of his earlier rowing activities.

After *Afloat* was published, Maupassant bought another boat, also called the *Bel-Ami*. This second one was bigger, a 14.6-metre yawl (formerly the *Zingara*). She had been built in 1879 in England, by Miller of Lymington, and was still owned by Maupassant when he was taken in to Dr Blanche's clinic in January 1892, eighteen months before his death on 6 July 1893 at almost forty-three. This *Bel-Ami* was often photographed and the advertisements for the eventual sale give many details, so the boat was quite well known. This was not true of the first *Bel-Ami*, which seems never to have been photographed; when Maupassant came to sell her he referred a prospective buyer to the accurate drawings that had been specially done for *Afloat* by E. Riou. Apart from these and his description in the book, there is little to go on, though some parts of the actual boat still exist: the map table, the compass and the solid brass tiller, all kept by the family of the last owner after she was broken up in 1904 (there is a plan to reconstruct the yacht).

His yachts, the *Bel-Ami*, Bernard, Raymond, the sea and the wind, were part of Maupassant's private life. Sailing became his escape from the world, and Maupassant the sailor is as important as Maupassant the writer in *Afloat*. Other sides of him are here as well – the ironical thinker, the humorist, the philosopher, the sensualist, the solitary, the convivial friend, the lover of women, the republican, the élitist, the nature-lover and the hunter of game.

Yet for more than a hundred years people have disagreed about Maupassant – the sensualist with an austere talent who was 'at once so licentious and so impeccable'; the 'courageous' man with the 'compassionate heart' who yet had no morals, 'an absence of scruple'. What was he really like, this man, a 'born sadist' with 'an eye of profound pity'? Among all Maupassant's works, *Afloat* is perhaps the nearest we are likely to get to his own answer. But was it really self-revelation? An extract from a letter to his publisher suggests it may have been: 'Concerning the manuscript, which is something I want to do very carefully, because it is full of very intimate thoughts, because it is my journal, it will take me all my time to get it ready. . . .' Yet Maupassant was not exactly noted for self-revelation (indeed quite the reverse). He did have a remarkable gift for observation and did not shirk from the conclusions he drew, and he had the courage, or perhaps the need, to extend this to self-analysis. Joseph Conrad wrote: 'He thinks sufficiently to concrete his fearless conclusions in illuminative instances. He renders them with that exact knowledge of the means and that absolute devotion to the aim of creating a true effect – which is art.'

Was *Afloat* art, or was it life? Maupassant felt strongly that the artist's work should be enough for the public; there was no need for his person also. But perhaps he deliberately revealed, in a veiled fashion, as much of the person as he was prepared to, through the medium of art. It is true that many of the feelings and thoughts expressed in *Afloat* are shared by thinkers of sensitivity and intelligence, for there are passages of a universality that surprises, delights and moves. But above everything else, it is Maupassant. It is full of his clear-sightedness, his common sense, his balance, his compassion.

ACKNOWLEDGEMENTS

The maps in this edition are reproduced with the kind
permission of
Éditions GALLIMARD, 1993
Collection Folio
Guy de MAUPASSANT, *Sur l'eau*
Édition présentée, établie et annotée par Jacques Dupont
(Professeur à l'Université de Nantes)

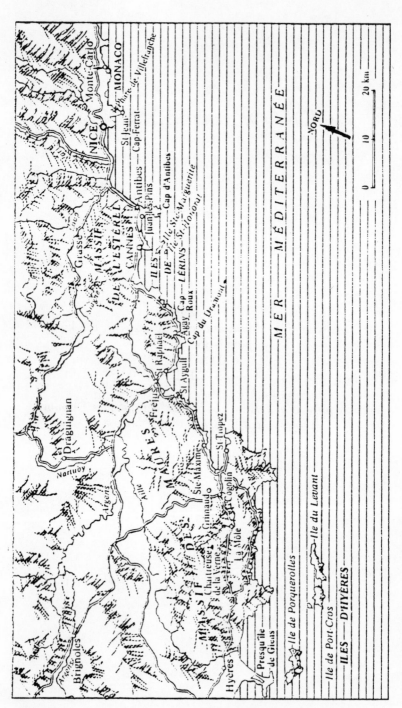

1. *The Côte d'Azur as Maupassant knew it*

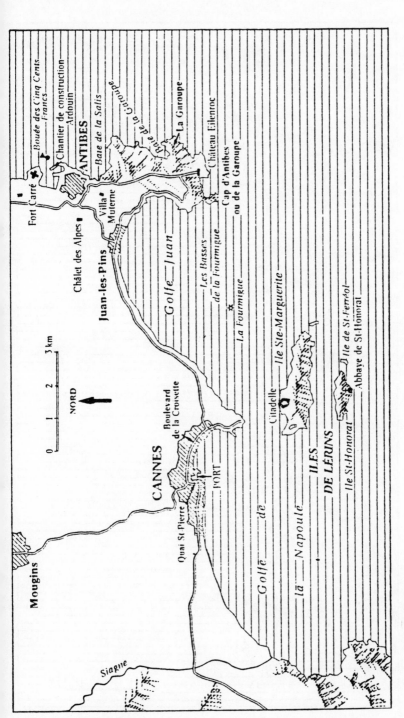

2. Cannes to Antibes

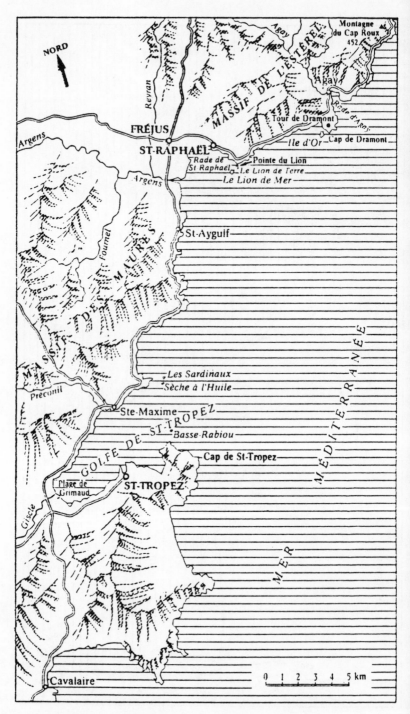

3. *Saint-Raphaël to Saint-Tropez*

This journal contains no interesting story or adventure. Having been, last spring, on a short cruise on the Mediterranean coast, I amused myself by writing down each day what I saw and what I thought.

In short, I saw water, sun, clouds and rocks – there is nothing else to tell – and I thought simply, as you think when the waves rock you, make you languid, and carry you on.

I was deeply asleep when Bernard, my skipper, threw sand up at my window. I opened it and felt the cold, refreshing night air on my face; I breathed it in and it almost entered my soul. The sky was clear, bluish and alive with the fiery twinkling of the stars.

The sailor, standing down by the wall, was saying, 'Fair weather, sir.'

'Where's the wind?'

'From the land.'

'Right, I'm coming.'

Half an hour later I was striding down to the sea. The horizon was beginning to get paler and I could see the lights of Nice in the distance, beyond the Bay of Angels; then, more distant still, the rotating beam of Villefranche lighthouse. Before me Antibes appeared vaguely in the clearing shadows, with its two towers standing up above the conical town, still enclosed in the old walls built by Vauban.

In the streets were a few dogs and a few men, some workmen getting up. In the port there was nothing but the slight rocking of the tartans* along the quay and the apathetic lapping

* Inshore fishing boats rigged as luggers, peculiar to the Mediterranean.

of the scarcely moving water; from time to time there was the noise of a tightening painter or the gentle rubbing of a boat against a hull. The boats, the pebbles, the very sea itself seemed asleep under the gold-dusted heavens and under the eye of the little lighthouse which, upright on the jetty, watched over its little port.

Across there, opposite Ardouin the boatbuilder's yard, I made out a light, sensed a movement, heard some voices; they were waiting for me. *Bel-Ami* was ready to sail.

I went down into the saloon, lit by two gimballed candles swinging like compasses at the foot of the long seats which served as a bed at night; I put on a leather jacket, put a warm cap on my head, then went back up to the cockpit. The moorings had already been cast off and the two men were heaving on the chain to bring the yacht directly over her anchor. Then they hoisted the mainsail, which rose slowly with a continuous squeaking from the blocks and the mast hoops; it rose up in the night, large and pale, hiding the sky and the stars and already moving slightly in the puffs of wind.

This was coming to us cold and dry from the still-invisible mountain, which we could sense was heavy with snow. The wind was very slight, scarcely awakened, indecisive and intermittent.

Now the men were bringing the anchor on board and I took the helm; the boat slipped over the still water like a great ghost. To leave the port we had to tack between the tartans and the slumbering schooners. We went from one quay to the other, gently, with our short, round dinghy following us as a newly hatched cygnet follows the swan.

As soon as we were in the channel between the jetty and the square fort the yacht, more eager, increased her speed and seemed to become more alive, as if a kind of gaiety had pervaded her; she was dancing on the countless light, low waves, moving furrows on an endless plain. She was sensing the life in the sea on leaving the dead water of the port.

As there was no swell I went between the town walls and Five Hundred Franc buoy which marks the main passage, then, letting the wind come aft, I set course to round the cape.

Dawn was breaking, the stars were disappearing, the Ville-franche lighthouse closed its rotating eye for the last time, and in the distant sky above Nice, which was still invisible, I could see a curious rosy glow; it was the Alpine glaciers, whose peaks were being lit up by the dawn.

I gave the helm to Bernard so that I could watch the sun rise. The gentle breeze, fresher now, was making us skim along the trembling, violet waves. A bell began to ring, sending out into the wind the three quick chimes of the angelus. Why is it that the sound of bells seems more brisk at daybreak and heavier at nightfall? I love this cold lightness of the morning, when men are still sleeping and the earth is waking up. The air is full of mysterious quiverings never experienced by those who lie late in their beds. You see, breathe, drink in the rebirth of life, the physical life of the world, that life which goes throughout the stars, whose secrets intrigue us immensely.

Raymond was saying: 'We'll soon have an east wind.'

Bernard replied: 'I'd think more likely from the west.'

Bernard, the skipper, is thin, easy-going, remarkably neat, careful and prudent; with a full beard, he has a straightfor-ward look, an agreeable voice and he is loyal and sincere. Yet when he is at sea everything worries him: meeting a sudden swell forecasting wind at sea; a cloud stretched out over the Esterel which shows that the mistral is in the west; and even a rising barometer, since it could be due to a sudden squall in the east. Though he is an excellent sailor; he watches over everything constantly and takes cleanliness so far that he rubs the brass the moment it is marked by a drop of water.

Raymond, his brother-in-law, is a strong fellow, dark, with a moustache, bold and untiring, as loyal and sincere as the other, but less highly strung and changeable, calmer, more re-signed to the treacheries and surprises of the sea.

Sometimes Bernard, Raymond and the barometer contradict each other and act out for me an amusing comedy with three characters – and the one with the non-speaking part knows the most.

'Good Lord, sir, we're going well,' said Bernard.

Indeed we had now passed the Bay of Salis, got by the

Garoupe, and were coming up to Cap Gros, a flat, low rock stretched out at wave level.

Now the whole chain of the Alps was appearing, a monstrous wave threatening the sea, a granite wave crowned with snow, whose pointed crests seemed like fixed and motionless jets of spray. The sun rose behind these frozen snows, and its light fell on them in a flood of silver.

Then, going round the Cap d'Antibes, we came upon the Îles de Lérins and, far beyond them, the twisted chain of the Esterel. The Esterel is the backdrop for Cannes, charming mountains from a print-album, bluish and elegantly jagged, done with an extravagant coquettishness and yet also with artistry, painted in watercolour on a theatrical sky by a good-humoured creator to be used as a model by the English landscape painters, and to be the object of admiration for the idle or consumptive nobility.

The Esterel changes its appearance every hour of the day and is greatly admired by the fashionable world.

The accurately and neatly drawn chain of mountains is outlined in the mornings against blue sky, pure and soft blue, a clean and pretty blue, the ideal blue of a southern beach. But in the evening the wooded slopes of the mountainside darken and make a black mark against a fiery sky, a sky which is improbably red and dramatic. I have never seen anywhere these fairy-tale sunsets, the entire horizon ablaze, these explosions of cloud, this skilful and superb scene setting, this daily renewal of magnificent and excessive effects which demand admiration and would produce a slight smile if they had been painted by man.

The Îles de Lérins, closing Cannes Bay to the east and separating it from the Golfe Juan, seem themselves to be two islands from an operetta, put there for the greater pleasure of the invalids and the winter visitors.

From the open sea, where we are now, they are like two dark green gardens, pushed into the water. Towards the sea at the far end of Saint-Honorat, rising straight out of the waves, is a completely romantic ruin, a real Sir Walter Scott castle continually battered by the waves, where long ago the monks defended themselves against the Saracens, for Saint-Honorat has always belonged to monks, except during the Revolution, for at that time the island was bought by an actress from the Théâtre-Français.

A fortified castle, battling monks, today's fat, smiling, alms-collecting Trappists, a pretty play-actress – coming no doubt to conceal her love affairs on this little island with its pines and its thickets, surrounded by a necklace of picturesque rocks – all of this, even the Florian style names 'Lérins, Saint-Honorat, Sainte-Marguerite', is pleasant, pretty, poetic, romantic and a little insipid on this delightful Cannes coastline.

To match the slender old crenellated castle, standing up at the far end of Saint-Honorat towards the open sea, Sainte-Marguerite ends on the landward side in the famous fortress where Bazaine and the Man in the Iron Mask were imprisoned. There is a channel about a mile wide between the point of La Croisette and this manor, which has the air of an old ruined house, with nothing aristocratic or majestic about it. It seems crouching, heavy and sombre, a real trap of a prison.

Now I can see the three bays. Before me, beyond the islands, is that of Cannes, a little nearer is the Golfe Juan, and behind me the Bay of Angels, dominated by the Alps with their snowy summits. Farther on the coast rolls on well beyond the Italian border, and through my telescope I discovered white Bordighera at the end of a cape.

Everywhere, all along this endless coastline, are towns at the edge of the water, villages perched higher up on the mountain-sides, and the innumerable villas scattered among the greenery have the air of white eggs laid on the sands, on the rocks, in the pine forests, by monstrous birds who come during the night from the snowy region which can be seen up above.

On the Cap d'Antibes, that long outgrowth of land, that fantastic garden thrown between two seas where the most beautiful flowers in Europe grow, we can see still more villas, and right at the end Eilen-Roc, that ravishing and imaginative dwelling to which visitors come from Nice and Cannes.

The wind is falling and the yacht is barely moving. After the air flow from the land which rules at night, we are waiting and hoping for a sea wind, welcome wherever it comes from.

Bernard still thinks it will come from the west, Raymond from the east; and the barometer is stationary at a little below 76°.

Now the sun is shining, flooding the land, making the walls of the houses sparkle – from the distance they look like scattered snow, and cast a clear, luminous bluish varnish over the sea.

Little by little, taking advantage of the slightest breeze, of those caresses of the air which are scarcely felt on the skin and yet make sensitive yachts with correctly set sails glide over the flat water, we are passing the last point of the headland and we can see the whole of the Golfe Juan, with the fleet in the middle.

From far off the battleships give the impression of rocks, little islands, reefs covered in dead trees. Steam from a train is running along the waterside, going from Cannes to Juan-les-Pins, which will perhaps later be the prettiest resort on the whole coast. Three tartans with their lateen sails, one red and the two others white, have stopped in the passage between Sainte-Marguerite and the land.

It is calm, the warm, gentle calm of a spring morning in the south; already it seems as though it was weeks, months, years ago that I left behind people who talk and become worked up; I can feel entering into me the rapture of being alone, the gentle rapture of a peace that nothing will disturb, no white letter, no blue telegram, not the sound of my door nor the barking of my dog. They cannot call to me, invite me, take me anywhere, oppress me with smiles or harass me with courtesy. I am alone, really alone, really free.

It is going fast, that steam from the train at the edge of the water; and I, I am floating in a winged, swaying lodging, pretty as a bird, small as a nest, more comfortable than a hammock, which wanders over the water, at the will of the wind, with nothing in particular in mind. I have two obedient sailors to look after me and take me everywhere, some books to read and stores for a fortnight. Two weeks without talking, what a delight!

I was closing my eyes in the heat of the sun, enjoying the

deep peace of the sea, when Bernard said quietly, 'The brig over there has some wind.'

Indeed over there, far off, opposite Agay, a brig is coming towards us. With the glasses I can clearly see her sails, round and full of wind.

'Humph! The wind is coming from Agay,' Raymond counters. 'It's calm at Cap Roux.'

'Say what you like, we'll have wind from the west,' replies Bernard.

I lean over to look at the barometer in the saloon. It has dropped in the last quarter of an hour. I say so to Bernard, who smiles and murmurs, 'It can feel the wind from the west, sir.'

That's it, my curiosity is awake, that special curiosity of sea voyagers, which makes them see everything, observe everything, makes them excited about the slightest thing. The glass no longer leaves my eyes and I watch the colour of the water on the horizon. It is still clear, glossy, shining; if there is any wind it is still far away.

What a character the wind is to sailors! They talk about it as of a man, of an all-powerful ruler, sometimes terrible, sometimes charitable. He is the one we discuss most, all day long; he is the one we think about incessantly, all day long and all night. You don't know him at all, you land-lubbers! It is we who know him better than our fathers and our mothers, this terrible, invisible, changeable, cunning, treacherous, ferocious person. We love him and we fear him, we know his tricks and his rages, which the signs in the sky and the sea slowly teach us to forecast. He makes us think about him every minute and every second, for the struggle between him and us never breaks off. Our whole being is alert for this battle – the eyes, which try to catch barely perceptible indications; the skin, which is caressed or buffeted; the mind, which recognizes his mood, forecasts his surprises, judges if he is calm or temperamental. No enemy, no woman, gives the feeling of battle, makes us take so many precautions as he does, for he is the master of the sea, he who can be used, avoided or fled from, but who can never be tamed. In a sailor's soul there reigns, just as in a believer's, the idea of an irascible and mighty God, the myste-rious, religious, never-ending fear of the wind, and respect for its power.

'There it is, sir,' Bernard says to me.

Over there, right over there on the far horizon, a blue-black line is spreading over the water. It is nothing, a nuance, an imperceptible shadow – there it is. Now we are waiting for it, motionless, in the heat of the sun.

I look at the time – eight o'clock – and I say, 'Damn it, it's early for a west wind.'

'It will blow hard after midday,' replies Bernard.

I raise my eyes to the flat, limp, dead sail. Its shining trian-gle seems to go up into the sky, as we have hoisted the big fair-weather topsail above the mainsail, and its jackyard goes two metres beyond the top of the mast. Not a movement: you could believe you were on land. The barometer is still falling. All the same, the dark line seen in the distance is getting nearer. The metallic gleam of the water, suddenly darker, becomes like slate. The sky is pure and cloudless.

Suddenly all around us, on a sea as clean as a steel plate, slipping here and there, quickly, gone as soon as they ap-pear, are imperceptible quivers, as though a thousand pinches of fine sand had been thrown on it. The sail trembles, but barely, and then slowly the boom moves to starboard. Now a breeze caresses my face and the trembling of the water is increasing all around us as though a continuous rain of sand were falling on it. The cutter is already moving again. She glides ahead and a very slight slapping starts all along her sides. The tiller stiffens in my hand, the long copper tiller which seems in the sun like a fiery wand, and the breath of wind is getting stronger second by second. We will have to go about, but what does it matter – the boat is pointing well into the wind and the wind, if it doesn't weaken, will take us tack by tack into Saint-Raphaël by nightfall.

We are coming up to the fleet, whose six battleships and two despatch boats are slowly turning on their anchors, pre-senting their bows to the west. Then we change tack out to sea to pass the Formigues, marked by a tower, in the middle of the bay. The wind is freshening more and more, surprisingly fast, and the waves are rising short and quickly. The yacht is heeling with full sail and running, still followed by the tender whose painter is tight and which, nose in the air and tail in the water, is going between two curls of spray.

Approaching the island of Saint-Honorat, we pass near a bare, red rock, spiny as a porcupine, so rough, armed with teeth, nails and claws that you can hardly walk on it; you have to put your feet in the hollows, between the defences, and go forward carefully. It is called Saint-Ferréol.

A little soil, come from goodness knows where, has built up in the holes and fissures in the rock, and in them have grown a kind of lily and charming blue irises, whose seeds seem to have fallen from the sky.

It was on this curious reef, out at sea, that the body of Paganini was entombed and hidden for five years. The adventure is worthy of the life of this gifted and macabre artist, who was said to be possessed by the devil, with so strange an appearance, of body and of face, and whose superhuman talent and exceptional thinness made him a legendary creature, a kind of Hoffmann character.

Just when he was returning to Genoa, his native land, accompanied by his son, the only one left who was able to hear him as his voice had become so weak, he died of cholera at Nice on 27 May 1840.

His son therefore put his father's body on a ship and left for Italy. But the Genoese clergy refused to give this demon a grave. The court of Rome was consulted and did not dare to give its authorization. All the same, they were going to put the body ashore when the city authorities opposed it on the grounds that the artist had died of cholera. At that time Genoa was ravaged by an epidemic of the disease, but they argued that the presence of another corpse could worsen the plague.

So Paganini's son returned to Marseilles, where he was not allowed to enter the port for the same reason. Then he went to Cannes, which he could not enter either. So he stayed at sea, with the waves rocking the corpse of the great and strange artist, whom men drove out from everywhere. He no longer knew what to do, where to go, where to take this body which was sacred to him, when he saw the bare rock of Saint-Ferréol in the middle of the waves. He had the coffin unloaded and it was buried in the middle of the islet.

It was only in 1845 that he came back with two friends to find his father's remains to take them to Genoa, to the Villa Gajona.

Wouldn't we have preferred the extraordinary violinist to have stayed on the spiny reef, where the waves sing in the strange gashes of the rock?

Farther on at sea the château of Saint-Honorat rises up, which we had seen as we rounded the cape of Antibes, and farther still a line of rocks ending in a tower: Les Moines.

At this moment they are all spray, whiteness and noise.

That is one of the most dangerous places on the coast at night, as no light marks it and shipwrecks are quite common.

A sudden gust makes us heel so that water comes up over the coaming and I give the order to take down the topsail, which the cutter can no longer carry without the risk of breaking the mast. The waves are deeper, more spaced out and foaming, and the wind whistles, raging, in squalls, a menacing wind, saying, 'Watch out.'

'We will have to go and stay the night at Cannes,' says Bernard.

Indeed, within half an hour we had to take down the number one jib and replace it with the number two, taking a reef in the mainsail; then, a quarter of an hour later, we were taking a second reef. So I decided to go in to the port of Cannes, a dangerous port with no shelter, roads open to the sea from the south-west which puts all the vessels in danger. When you think of the considerable sums which big foreign yachts would bring to the town if they were to find safe shelter, you can appreciate the power of indolence in the people of the Midi, who have still not managed to get this essential work out of the state.

At ten o'clock we drop anchor opposite the steamer *Le Cannois*, and I go ashore, upset at this interrupted voyage. The whole harbour is white with foam.

Cannes, 7 April, 9 p.m.

Princes, princes, princes everywhere! Those who love princes are happy here. Yesterday morning I had scarcely put my foot on the promenade of La Croisette but I met three of them, one behind the other. In our democratic country Cannes has become a town of titles.

If you could open minds as you lift the lid of a saucepan, you would find numbers in the head of a mathematician; silhouettes of gesturing and declaiming actors in the head of a playwright; a woman's face in the head of a man in love; bawdy pictures in that of a rake; verses in the brain of a poet; but in the skulls of people who come to Cannes, you would find every variety of crown, swimming like pasta in soup.

Some men meet in gaming dens because they love cards, others at racecourses because they love horses. People meet in Cannes because they love Imperial and Royal Highnesses, who are at home there, reigning peacefully over loyal salons for lack of the kingdoms that have been taken away from them. You meet them, great and small, rich and poor, gay and sad, to all tastes. In general they are modest, seek to please and bring a delicacy and an affability to their relations with humble mortals which you almost never find in our deputies, those princes of the ballot box.

Though if these princes, these poor wandering princes with no budget or subjects, who come to live like bourgeois in this elegant town full of flowers, appear to be simple and give no cause for mirth, even to the disrespectful, it is not the same thing with the lovers of royalty. These people circulate round their idols with a religious and comic assiduity, and as soon as they are deprived of one, set out in search of another, as if their mouth can only open to pronounce 'Monseigneur' or 'Madame' in the third person.

You cannot see them for more than five minutes without their telling you what the Princess replied to them, what the Grand Duke told them, the walk planned with one, the witty remark of another. You feel, you guess, you see that they do not frequent any world other than that of persons of royal blood, and that if they consent to speak to you it is to inform you about exactly what is done at these heights.

Some desperate battles begin, battles in which all imaginable tricks are used in order to have at their table, at least once a season, a prince, a real prince, one of those who are at a premium. What respect is inspired when they go to the lawn-tennis party of a grand duke, or when they have even been presented to 'Wales' – that is the expression of the *superchics*.

To leave their name at the door of these 'exiles', as Daudet says, of those who were kicked out, another might say, amounts to a major occupation, constant, delicate and absorbing. The book is placed in the entrance hall between two valets, one of whom offers a pen. They write their name after two thousand other names of every feather, where titles flourish, where the '*de*' is abundant! Then off they go, proud as if they had just been ennobled, happy as if they had just accomplished a holy duty, and they say with pride to the first acquaintance encountered, 'I have just been to leave my name at the Grand Duke of Gérolstein's.' Then in the evening, at dinner, they say with a weighty air, 'I noticed just now, on the list at the Grand Duke of Gérolsteins's, the names of X ... Y ... and Z ....' And everyone listens with interest as if it were an event of major importance.

Though why laugh and be astonished at the innocent and gentle obsession of these elegant lovers of princes, when in Paris fifty different species of fanciers of great men are to be encountered, no less amusing.

For anyone with a salon, it is essential to be able to show celebrities, and a hunt is organized for their conquest. There is hardly a society woman, and of the best society, who is not bent on having her artist, or her artists, and she gives dinners for them to make it clear, in town and country, that there is intellect at her house.

Pretending to have a mind you do not have but which you obtain with a great flourish, or having princely acquaintances – what is the difference?

The most sought-after among great men, by women young or old, are certainly musicians. Some houses have complete collections of them. Besides, these artists have the immeasurable advantage of being useful at receptions. But people who go for the really rare object can scarcely hope to have two of them together on the same sofa. One might add that there are no depths to which a well-known, prominent woman will not sink to decorate her salon with a famous composer. The minor efforts normally used to attract an artist or a simple man of letters become totally inadequate when it is a matter of a seller of sounds. In his case means of seduction and methods of praise are used which are completely unheard of. His hands are kissed like a king, he is knelt to like a god when he himself has deigned to perform his *Regina Coeli*. A hair of his beard is worn in a ring, a medallion, a sacred medallion on the end of a little gold chain kept between the breasts, is made from a button which fell from his trousers one evening after a quick movement of the arms which he made as he finished his *Doux Repos*.

Artists are a little less prized, although still very much sought-after. They have in them a little less of the divine and more of the bohemian. Their manner does not have enough smoothness and is certainly not sufficiently elevated. They often replace inspiration with irrelevancies and revelry. They have rather too much of a smell of the studio in fact, and those who by making an effort have lost that smell, begin to seem like poseurs. And then they are changeable, flighty, mocking. You are never sure of keeping them, while the musician makes his nest in the family.

For several years the man of letters has been quite sought-after. He has, moreover, great advantages: he talks, he talks a long time, he talks a great deal, he talks on behalf of everyone, and since he makes intelligence his profession, you can listen to him and admire him with confidence.

The woman who feels motivated by this bizarre taste for having a man of letters in her house, as you might have a parrot whose talking attracts the neighbouring concierges, has a choice between poets and novelists. Poets have more idealism, and novelists more of the impromptu. Poets are more sentimental, novelists more positive. It's a matter of taste and temperament. The poet has a more intimate charm, the novelist often more wit. But the novelist presents dangers that are not found in the poet: he consumes, pillages and exploits everything before his eyes. You can never feel comfortable with him, never be sure that he will not put you into bed one day, quite naked, between the pages of a book. His eye is like a pump which sucks up everything, like the hand of a thief always at work. Nothing escapes him, he gathers and picks up incessantly; he gathers movements, gestures, intentions, everything before him which happens or is happened upon; he picks up the slightest things, the slightest words, the slightest deeds. From morning to night he stores up observations of every kind out of which he makes stories to sell, stories that go to the ends of the earth, which will be read, argued about, commented on by thousands and millions of people. And what is terrible is that he will make it lifelike, the rogue, unable to help it, unconsciously, because he sees correctly and he tells of what he has seen. In spite of his efforts and ruses to disguise the characters, people say, 'Did you recognize Mr X . . . and Madame Y . . .? They are striking.'

Certainly it is as dangerous for society people to attract and indulge novelists as it would be for a flour merchant to raise rats in his store.

And yet they are in favour.

Consequently when a woman has designs on the writer she wants to take up, she lays siege by using attentions, treats and compliments. Like water which, drop by drop, will get through the hardest rock, the praise, word by word, enters the sensitive heart of the man of letters. Then, as soon as she sees him softened, moved, won by this constant flattery, she isolates him, she cuts, little by little, the ties he could have elsewhere, and accustoms him, without his noticing, to come to her, to find it pleasing there, to lodge his thought there. To make him thoroughly acclimatized to her house, she arranges and makes the most of his successes, shows him off to advantage, as an attraction, and in front of all the old regulars she shows him particular attention, unparalleled admiration.

So, feeling he is an idol, he stays in this temple. Besides, he finds it is to his advantage, since the other women attempt their most delicate favours to snatch him from the one who has conquered him. Though if he is skilful, he will not succumb to the charms and invitations with which he is heaped, and the more he shows that he is faithful, the more he will be pursued, entreated, loved. Oh! he should beware letting himself be carried off by all these sirens of the salons; he would immediately lose three-quarters of his value if he went into circulation.

He soon becomes a literary group, a church in which he is God, the only God, because real religions never have several divinities. People go to the house to see him, hear him, admire him, as people come from far away to certain sanctuaries. They will envy him, they will envy her! They will talk about literature as priests talk about dogmas, knowledgeably and seriously; they will be listened to, he and she, and as they leave this literary salon, people will have the feeling of leaving a cathedral.

Others too are sought-after, but to a lesser degree; thus generals, disdained in real society where they are classified as scarcely above government deputies, are still at a premium in the lower-middle classes. A deputy is only required at moments of crisis. He is kept going, with a dinner from time to time, during periods of parliamentary calm. Scholars have their partisans, since in nature all tastes exist, and the chief clerk himself is much appreciated by people who live on the sixth floor. But these people do not come to Cannes. The middle classes have but a few timid representatives there.

It is only before midday that all the noble foreigners can be met on La Croisette.

La Croisette is a long semi-circular promenade which follows the sea from the promontory opposite Sainte-Marguerite as far as the port, commanded by the old town.

Young and slim women – it is good taste to be thin – dressed in the English style, are walking at a brisk pace, escorted by alert young men in tennis clothes. Though from time to time you come across a poor emaciated creature dragging himself along with weary steps, leaning on the arm of a mother, a brother or a sister. They cough and gasp, these poor wretches, enveloped in shawls despite the heat, and watch us passing by with miserable, profound, desperate eyes.

They are suffering, they are dying, for this warm and ravishing region is also society's hospital and the European aristocracy's cemetery.

The dreadful illness from which recovery is rare and which today they call tuberculosis, the illness which eats away, consumes and destroys men in thousands, seems to have chosen this coast to finish off its victims.

How it must be cursed in all the corners of the earth, this charming and dangerous land, death's pleasant and scented antechamber, where so many families, royal and humble, princely and bourgeois, have left someone behind, almost always a child, the object of their burgeoning hopes and their increasing affection.

I recall Menton, the warmest, the healthiest of these winter resorts. In the same way that in towns of military importance you see fortresses up on the surrounding heights, so from this beach of the dying you catch sight of the cemetery at the top of a little hill.

What a place it would be to live, this garden where the dead sleep! Roses, roses, there are roses everywhere. They are blood red, or pale, or white, or veined with scarlet. The tombs, the paths, the places empty today and filled tomorrow, everything is covered with them. Their incredibly strong perfume is overwhelming, making head and legs unsteady.

All those who are lying there were sixteen, eighteen, twenty years old. From tomb to tomb you go, reading the names of these creatures who were killed so young by incurable disease. It is a cemetery of children, like the white balls where married people are not allowed.

From this cemetery the view extends on the left to Italy, as far as the headland where Bordighera stretches out its white houses to the sea, to the right as far as Cap Martin, which dips its leafy slopes into the water.

Everywhere, moreover, along the length of this lovely coastline, we are in the presence of Death. But it is discreet, veiled, all good manners and modesty, well-brought-up, in fact. You will never see it face to face, even though it brushes by you all the time.

You could even say that people do not die in this area, for everything conspires with the fraud which this sovereign delights in. But how you can feel it, how you can catch its scent, how you can sometimes glimpse the end of its black robe! Certainly plenty of roses are needed and plenty of lemon blossom, so that you never catch in the breeze the frightful smell that drifts from the rooms of the departed.

There is never a coffin in the streets, never a funeral pall, never a tolling bell. Yesterday's thin walker no longer passes beneath your window, and that is all.

If you are surprised not to see him and are concerned about him, the head waiter and all the servants reply with a smile that he was getting better, and that on the doctor's advice he has left for Italy. Indeed in every hotel Death has its secret staircase, its confidants and its accomplices.

A moralist of former times would have some very fine things to say about the juxtaposition and the contrast of this elegance and this misery.

It was midday, the promenade was empty and I returned on board the *Bel-Ami*, where a modest lunch was waiting for me, prepared by Raymond, whom I found in a white apron frying the potatoes.

I read for the rest of the day.

The wind was still blowing violently and the yacht was dancing on its anchors, for we had had to drop the starboard one too. The movement eventually made me drowsy and I dozed off for a while. When Bernard came into the saloon to light the candles I saw that it was already seven o'clock, and since the swell all along the quay made disembarkment difficult, I dined on my boat.

Afterwards I went on deck to sit in the open air. All around me Cannes was spreading its lights. There is nothing prettier than the lights of a town seen from the sea. To the left, the old quarter, whose houses seem to climb up one on top of the other, was going on to mingle its lights with the stars; to the right, the gas lights of La Croisette were unwinding like an immense snake which extended for two kilometres.

Then I thought that in all these villas, in all these hotels, people are gathered together this evening, as they were yesterday, as they will be tomorrow, and they are talking. They are talking! About what? About princes! The weather! And then? The weather! Princes! And then? Nothing!

Is there anything more calamitous than the conversation at a hotel dinner table? I have stayed in hotels, I have been subjected to the human mind which appears there in all its platitude. You really have to be quite determined on supreme indifference so as not to cry with shame, grief and disgust when you hear men talking. Man, ordinary man, rich, well known, liked, respected, circumspect, self-satisfied, he knows nothing, understands nothing and talks about intelligence with an arrogance that makes one despair.

You would need to be blind and drunk with stupid pride to believe yourself to be anything but a beast scarcely superior to others! Listen to them, sitting round the table, these poor creatures! They are talking! They are talking gently, confidently, ingenuously, and they call that the exchange of ideas. What ideas? They tell you where they have been for a walk: 'The road was very pretty, but it was a little chilly on the way back'; 'The cooking is not bad in the hotel, though restaurant food is always a little rich'. And they relate what they have done, what they like, what they believe.

It seems to me that in them I see the horror of their mind just as you see a foetal monster in alcohol in a specimen jar. I watch the slow hatching of the commonplaces they are always repeating, I feel the words falling down from this storehouse of idiocies into their foolish mouths and from their mouths into the inert air which carries them to my ears.

But their ideas, their most respected, most solemn, most lofty ideas, are they not the unchallengeable proof of universal, eternal, indestructible and all-powerful stupidity?

All their conceptions of God, the clumsy god who went wrong with the first creatures and began again, who hears our confidences and takes note of them, the god who is policeman, Jesuit, lawyer, gardener, in armour, robed or sandalled. Then there are the denials of God based on earthly logic, the arguments for and against, the history of religious belief, of schisms, of heresies, of philosophies, the affirmations like the doubts, all the puerility of principles, the ferocious and bloody violence of those with hypotheses, the chaos of the confrontations. All the miserable effort of this unhappy creature who lacks the power to conceive, to guess, to know, and yet is so swift to believe, all this proves that men have been cast into this little world solely to eat, drink, have children, sing songs and kill each other to pass the time.

Happy are those who are satisfied with life, those who are amused by it, those who are content.

There are people who like everything, who are charmed by everything. They love the sun and the rain, the snow and the fog, the calm of their home and celebrations, everything they see, everything they do, everything they say, everything they hear. These people live a tranquil, gentle and satisfied life in the middle of their offspring, and those have a lively existence of pleasures and distractions. Neither one nor the other is bored. Life for them is a sort of amusing spectacle in which they are themselves actors, a good and changing thing which, without surprising them too much, delights them.

Other men though, in a flash of thought running round the

circle of possible satisfactions, remain appalled at the futility of happiness, the monotony and the poverty of terrestrial joys. As soon as they reach thirty everything is over for them. What are they waiting for? Nothing interests them any more; they have gone the round of our meagre pleasures.

Happy are those who do not know the terrible nausea of the same actions always repeated; happy are those who have the strength to begin again each day the same tasks, with the same gestures, around the same pieces of furniture, before the same horizon, under the same sky, to go out into the same streets where they meet the same faces and the same animals. Happy are those who do not notice with immense disgust that nothing changes, nothing passes and that all is vanity.

We would have to have a mind that is slow, closed and undemanding to be content with what is. How is it that the world public has not yet cried 'Curtain!', has not demanded the next act with creatures other than man, other shapes, other celebrations, other plants, other stars, other inventions, other adventures?

Can it be true that no one has yet felt hatred of the human face which is always the same, hatred of animals which seem like living mechanisms with their unvarying instincts transmitted in their seed from the first of their race to the last, hatred of landscapes eternally the same, and hatred of pleasures never renewed?

Take consolation, they say, in a love of science and the arts.

Do they not then see that we are always imprisoned in ourselves, beyond reach of escape, condemned to the ball and chain of our earthbound dreams!

The entire progress of our cerebral effort consists of the observation of physical facts by means of ridiculously imperfect instruments, which nevertheless slightly make up for the deficiencies of our organs. Every twenty years, a poor researcher who dies in want discovers that the air contains a gas that is still unknown; that a weightless, unanalysable, indescribable force is released by rubbing wax on cloth; that among the innumerable unknown stars there happens to be one that has not yet been recorded in the vicinity of another, which was seen and named long ago. What does it matter?

Our illnesses come from microbes – agreed. But where do these microbes come from? and the illnesses of these invisible beings themselves? And the suns, where do they come from?

We know nothing, we see nothing, we can do nothing, we can guess at nothing, we can imagine nothing, we are closed in, imprisoned in ourselves. And people marvel at human genius!

The arts? Painting consists of the reproduction in colour of monotone landscapes without their ever resembling nature; of drawing men, in trying without ever succeeding to give them the look of the living. Artists slave away like that, uselessly, for years, imitating what exists and, with this motionless and dumb copy of the acts of life, they scarcely succeed in making the trained eye understand what they were trying to do.

Why this effort? Why this vain imitation? Why this banal reproduction of things so sad in themselves? It is pitiful!

Poets do with words what artists attempt with colours. Yet why?

When you have read the four most skilful, the four most ingenious, it is pointless opening another. You will know nothing more. These men, too, can only imitate man. They wear themselves out in sterile labour. Since man does not change, their useless art is immutable. From the first stirrings of our limited thought, man is the same, his perceptions, beliefs, feelings are the same, he has not advanced, he has not regressed, he has not moved. What use is it to me to learn what I am, to read what I think, to see myself in the banal adventures of a novel?

Ah! if poets could travel through space, explore the stars, discover other universes, other beings, unceasingly vary the nature and the form of things for my mind, unceasingly take me into a changing and surprising unknown, open mysterious doors on to unexpected and marvellous horizons, I would read them night and day. But, impotently, they can only change the place of a word, and show me my image, as the artists do. To what end?

Because man's thought is immobile.

Once precise, near, unbreachable limits are reached, it goes round like a horse in a circus, like a fly in a closed bottle flying to the edges, which it always bumps into.

And yet, when there is nothing better to do, it is pleasant to think, when you live alone.

On this little sea-tossed boat, which a wave can fill and overturn, I know and I can feel how the things we know about are as nothing, for the earth floating in a void is even more isolated, more lost than this barque on the waves. Their importance is the same, their destiny will come about. I am glad I comprehend the emptiness of belief and the vanity of the hopes that are engendered by our insect-like pride!

I went to bed, rocked by the pitching, and I slept deeply as you do sleep afloat until the moment when Bernard woke me to tell me: 'Bad weather, sir, we can't leave this morning.'

The wind had dropped, but there was a heavy swell out at sea, making it impossible to head for Saint-Raphaël.

Another day to be spend in Cannes.

Towards midday there was a west wind again, less strong than the day before, and I decided to make use of it to go and visit the fleet in the Golfe Juan.

The *Bel-Ami*, as she crossed the bay, was leaping like a goat and I had to helm most carefully so as not to get sheets of water thrown in my face with every wave, as they were almost coming at us broadside. Soon though, I was in the lee of the islands and I headed for the passage beneath the fortified castle of Sainte-Marguerite.

Its right-hand wall drops down to the sea-battered rocks, and its top scarcely reaches above the low slope of the island. It had the air of a head thrust down between two big shoulders.

You can easily see the spot where Bazaine* got down. There was no need to be a skilled gymnast to let yourself slide down these accommodating rocks.

This escape was told to me in great detail by a man who claimed to be, and who could have been, well informed.

Bazaine was living quite freely, being visited each day by his wife and children. However, Madame Bazaine, a forceful character, told her husband that she would go away for ever with

* In 1873 Marshal Bazaine was sentenced to death for surrendering Metz during the Franco-Prussian War, but the sentence was commuted to imprisonment for 20 years. He escaped in August 1874.

her children if he did not get out, and she told him her plan. He hesitated at the dangers of the escape and the doubtfulness of its success; but when he saw that his wife was determined to carry out her threat, he agreed.

So every day children's toys were brought into the fortress, a complete, minute indoor gymnasium. It was from these toys that they made the knotted rope which the Marshal was to use. It was made slowly, so as not to arouse suspicion, then carefully hidden in a corner of the prison yard by a friendly hand.

Then the day of the escape was fixed. They chose a Sunday, as supervision seemed less strict on that day, and Madame Bazaine stayed away for a while.

The Marshal generally walked about in the prison yard until eight o'clock in the evening, in the company of the governor, a friendly man with whom he got on well. Then he would go to his rooms, which the head gaoler would bolt and padlock in the presence of his senior.

On the evening of the escape, Bazaine pretended to be unwell and wanted to go in an hour earlier. He did go in to his apartments, but as soon as the governor had gone off to find his gaoler and to warn him to shut up the prisoner immediately, the Marshal very quickly went out again and hid in the courtyard.

They locked the empty prison. Then each of them returned to his quarters.

About eleven o'clock Bazaine came out of his hiding place armed with the ladder. He made it fast and went down on to the rocks.

As dawn broke an accomplice undid the rope and threw it to the bottom of the wall.

Towards half-past eight the governor of Sainte-Marguerite enquired after the prisoner, surprised that he had not yet seen him, since he used to go out early every morning. Bazaine's valet refused to go in to his master.

Eventually, at nine o'clock, the governor forced the door and found the cage empty.

Madame Bazaine meanwhile, to carry out her plan, had found a man to whom her husband had formerly been of very great service. She approached a grateful heart and made an ally as devoted as he was determined. They arranged all the details together, then she went to Genoa under a false name and chartered a little Italian steamer at a thousand francs a day, with the pretence of an excursion to Naples, stipulating that the voyage would last at least a week and that it could be prolonged for the same period with the same conditions.

The vessel set out; but hardly had they put to sea when the traveller seemed to change her mind, and she asked the captain if he would mind going as far as Cannes to fetch her sister-in-law. The sailor willingly agreed and they dropped anchor, on Sunday evening, in the Golfe Juan.

Madame Bazaine had herself put ashore, ordering that the dinghy should not leave. Her devoted accomplice was waiting for her with another boat on the promenade of La Croisette, and they crossed the channel which separates the mainland from the little isle of Sainte-Marguerite. Her husband was there on the rocks, his clothes torn, his face battered, his hands bloodstained. Since the sea was rather heavy he was obliged to enter the water to reach the boat, which would have been damaged against the coast.

When they got back to land that boat was abandoned.

They returned to the first boat, and then to the still-steaming vessel. Madame Bazaine declared to the captain that her sister-in-law was too unwell to come and, indicating the Marshal, she added, 'Since I have no servant, I have taken a valet. This idiot has just fallen on the rocks and got himself into the state you can see. Please send him off with the crew, and see he is given what he needs to dress his wounds and sew up his clothes.'

Bazaine went to sleep between decks.

However, the next day, at daybreak, they had got out to sea. Once more Madame Bazaine changed her plans and, saying she was ill, had them take her back to Genoa.

But the news of the escape was already known and the people, aware of it, rose up shouting beneath the windows of the house. The tumult soon became so violent that the landlord, alarmed, got the travellers to slip away through a secret door.

I offer this story as it was told to me, and I can confirm nothing.

*

We were coming up to the fleet, whose heavy battleships, all in line, seemed like fortified towers constructed out at sea. Here are the *Colbert*, the *Devastation*, the *Amiral-Duperré*, the *Courbet*, the *Indomptable* and the *Richelieu*, then two cruisers, the *Hirondelle* and the *Milan*, and four torpedo boats on manoeuvres in the bay.

I wanted to visit the *Courbet*, which is said to be the most perfect of its kind in our navy.

Nothing conveys the idea of human labour, of the meticulous and fearsome labour of this little creature with clever hands, as do these enormous steel fortresses which float and advance, which carry an army of soldiers, an arsenal of monstrous weapons, and which are constructed, these massive objects, of little pieces fitted, bolted, forged, welded together, the work of ants and of giants, showing at one and the same time all the genius and all the impotence and all the irremediable barbarity of this race, so active and so weak, which wears itself out in creating machines for self-destruction.

The men of former times, who built cathedrals of lace out of stone, fairytale palaces as a shelter for childlike and pious dreams, were they not of the value of these of today, who launch into the sea steel houses which are temples of death?

Just as I was leaving the ship to climb back into my cockleshell, I heard the explosion of a fusillade from the shore. It was the Antibes regiment doing shooting exercises on the sand and among the pine trees. The smoke ascended in white wisps, like cotton clouds evaporating, and you could see the red trousers of the soldiers running along by the sea.

Then the naval officers, interested all of a sudden, turned their telescopes towards the land and their hearts lifted at this simulated war.

When I only think of that word, war, I feel as appalled as if it were a question of witchcraft, of inquisition, of something far-off, ended, unspeakable, monstrous, against nature.

When we talk about cannibals we have a proud smile as we proclaim our superiority over these savages. Who are the savages, the real savages? Those who fight each other to eat the vanquished, or those who fight each other to kill, just to kill?

The little infantrymen running about over there are destined for death just like the flocks a butcher drives along the roads. They will go and fall on the plain, their head split by a sabre blow or with a ball in the chest, and these are young men who could have worked, produced, been useful. Their fathers are old and poor, their mothers, who have loved and adored them for twenty years, as mothers do adore, will learn in six months or a year perhaps that their son, their child, their big child brought up with so much trouble, so much money, so much love, was thrown in a hole like a dead dog, after being gutted by a bullet and trampled on, crushed, reduced to pulp by cavalry charges. Why have they killed her boy, her lovely boy, her only hope, her pride, her life? She doesn't know. Yes, why?

War! Fighting! Butchery! The massacre of men! And we have today, in our time, with our civilization, with the breadth of knowledge and the degree of philosophy which we suppose the human mind to have attained, we have schools where they learn to kill, to kill from far away, perfectly, many people at the same time, to kill poor devils of innocent men, who have family responsibilities and no criminal records.

And the most astounding thing is that the people do not rise up against the government. What, then, is the difference between a monarchy and a republic? The most astounding thing is that the entire community does not rebel at the word 'war'.

Ah! we will always live with the burden of the old and odious ways, the culpable prejudice, the ferocious ideas of our barbarian ancestors, because we are beasts, will remain beasts, ruled by instinct, and which nothing will change.

Would not anyone other than Victor Hugo have been reviled if they had raised this great cry of release and truth?

'Today, force is called violence and its judgement is beginning; war is being accused. Civilization, with the human race as plaintiff, is preparing the trial and mounting the great criminal case against the conquerors and the captains. The people will come to understand that amplifying atrocities cannot diminish them; that if to kill is a crime, killing large numbers cannot be an attenuating factor; that if to steal is shameful, invasion cannot be glory.... Ah! let us proclaim these absolute truths, let us dishonour war.'

Vain anger, the indignation of a poet. War is more venerated than ever.

A skilled artist in this respect, Monsieur de Moltke,* responded one day to peace delegates with these strange words: 'War is holy, divinely instituted; it is one of the sacred laws of the world; it keeps alive in men all the great and noble ideas, honour, detachment, virtue, courage, and prevents them, in a word, from falling into the most hideous materialism.'

So, to join a pack of four hundred thousand men, march night and day without rest, think about nothing, learn or study nothing, read nothing, be of use to no one, rot in filth, sleep in muck, live like perpetually stupefied brutes, pillage towns, burn villages, ruin the population, then meet another great mass of human meat, hurl yourself at it, make lakes of blood, plains of pounded flesh mixed with muddied and reddened earth, heaps of corpses, have arms or legs taken off, your brain reduced to pulp to no purpose, and die in a corner of a field while your old parents, your wife and your children die of hunger; that is what is called not falling into the most hideous materialism!

Men of war are a plague on the world. We struggle against nature, ignorance, against obstacles of every kind, to make our miserable life less hard. Men, benefactors, scientists, wear out their existence with work, in searching for what might help, succour or relieve their brothers. They go on, bent on their useful work, amassing discoveries, enlarging the human spirit, increasing science, each day adding a sum of new knowledge to the intellect, each day giving their country well-being, comfort, power.

War comes. In six months the generals have destroyed twenty years of effort, patience and genius.

That is what is called not falling into the most hideous materialism.

* Chief of the Prussian General Staff (also Field Marshal, then Count) and architect of the Prussian victories against Denmark in 1864, Austria in 1866 and France in 1871.

War – we have seen it. We have seen men becoming brutes, driven mad, killing for pleasure, from terror, from bravado, from exhibitionism. When rights no longer exist, when the law is dead, when all notion of justice has disappeared, we have seen the shooting of innocent people, found on a road and becoming suspect because they were frightened. We have seen the killing of dogs chained to their master's door to try out a new revolver, we have seen cows lying in a field filled with shot for pleasure, without any reason, to make the gun fire, for fun.

That is what is called not falling into the most hideous materialism.

To enter a country, cut the throat of the man who is defending his house because he is wearing an overall and has no peaked cap on his head, burn the homes of wretches who have no more bread, break the pieces of furniture, steal others, drink the wine found in the cellars, rape the women found in the streets, burn millions of francs to dust, and leave behind misery and cholera.

That is what is called not falling into the most hideous materialism.

What have they done then, the men of war, to prove even a little intelligence? Nothing. What have they invented. Guns and cannons. That is all.

Has not the inventor of the wheelbarrow done more for man, with the simple and practical idea of fitting a wheel to two pieces of wood, than the inventor of modern fortifications?

What remains of Greece? Books, marbles. Was it great from what it conquered or what it produced?

Was it the invasion of the Persians that prevented it from falling into the most hideous materialism?

Was it the barbarian invasions that saved and regenerated Rome?

Did Napoleon I continue the great intellectual movement started by the philosophers at the end of the last century?

Well in a way, yes; since governments thus assume the power to put the people to death, there is nothing surprising in the people sometimes assuming the power to put governments to death.

They are defending themselves, they are right. No one has the absolute right to govern others. It can only be done for the good of those governed. Whoever governs has a duty to avoid war just as a captain of a ship has that of avoiding shipwreck. When a captain has lost his vessel he is judged, and he is condemned if he is seen to be guilty of negligence or even of incompetence.

Why are governments not judged after each war which is declared? If the people understood that, if they themselves administered justice to the murdering powers, if they refused to let themselves be killed without reason, if the people used their arms against those who provided them for slaughter, on that day war would be dead. . . . But that day will not come!

'Good weather, sir.'

I got up and went on deck. It was three o'clock in the morning; the sea was flat, the endless sky was like an immense shadowy vault scattered with fiery seeds. A very light breeze was blowing from the land.

The coffee was hot, we drank it, and without losing a minute, so as to make the most of this favourable wind, we left.

We were there, slipping over the waves, out to sea. The coast was disappearing; we could no longer see anything around us but blackness. That was a disturbing and delightful feeling, an emotion – plunging into that empty night, in that silence, over that water, far from everything. It seemed like leaving the world behind, that you never have to arrive anywhere, that there will be no more shore, that there will be no day. At my feet a little lantern lit the compass which showed me the way. We had to sail at least three miles out to sea to be sure of passing Cap Roux and the Dramont, whichever wind blew when the sun came up. I had the navigation lights lit, red to port and green to starboard, to avoid accidents, and I was elated by this peaceful, continuous and silent flight.

All at once there was a shout in front of us. It made me jump, for the voice was close, and I saw nothing, nothing but this dark wall of shadows into which I was plunging and which closed up again behind me. Raymond, on watch at the bow, said to me, 'It's a tartan going east; bear away a bit, sir, we will go astern.'

Then suddenly, right by us, a vague and alarming ghost rose up, the great floating shadow of a tall sail seen for a few seconds and gone almost at once. Nothing is more strange, more fantastic and more moving than these sudden apparitions at sea, at night. The fishermen and the sand dredgers never carry lights, so you only see them as you almost touch them, and that leaves you with the sense of a heart-clutching supernatural encounter.

Far-off I heard the whistle of a bird. It came near, passed and went away. Why can't I wander like that!

At last dawn appeared, slowly and gently, without a cloud, and the day followed it, a real summer day.

Raymond declared we would have an east wind, Bernard still stuck to the west and advised me to change course and go on the starboard tack towards the Dramont, which was rising up in the distance. I followed his advice at once and, with the slow push of a dying breath of wind, we approached the Esterel. The long red coastline falls into the blue water, making it seem violet. It is bizarre, spiny, pretty, with innumerable bays and headlands, fanciful and captivating rocks, a thousand fantastic forms of these much admired mountains. On the slopes, forests of pines climb to granite summits, which are like châteaux, towns, armies of stones running one after the other, and the sea is so clear at the foot that in places you can see the sandy bottom and the stems of the plants.

It is true that, on certain days, I feel the horror of what exists, to the point of wishing to be dead. I sense to the point of acute pain the unchanging monotony of the landscape, of faces and of thoughts. The mediocrity of the universe astonishes and repels me, the pettiness of everything fills me with disgust, the inadequacy of human beings overwhelms me.

On other days, on the contrary, I take an animal pleasure in everything. If my agitated, unquiet mind, overstretched by work, leaps at hopes which are not for our race, and then falls back into contempt for everything, having seen the emptiness of it all, my animal body is elated by all the ecstasies of life. I love the sky like a bird, the forests like a prowling wolf, the rocks like a chamois, the long grass to roll in, run over like a horse, and the clear water to swim in like a fish. I feel quivering in me something of all the species of animal, something of all the instincts, all the confused desires of the lower creatures. I love the earth as they do and not like you, men, I love it without admiration, without excitement, without being poetical. I love with a bestial and profound love, both base and sacred, everything that lives, everything that grows, everything you can see, because all of that, while leaving my mind calm, stirs my eyes and my heart, everything – the days, the nights, rivers, seas, tempests, woods, dawns, the gaze and the flesh of women.

The caress of the water on the sandy banks or on the granite of the rocks moves and softens me, and the joy that overwhelms me when I can feel myself pushed by the wind and carried by the waves, comes from my giving myself up to the brutal and natural forces of the world, my going back to a primitive life.

When the weather is fine like today, I have the blood of vagabond and lascivious fauns in my veins, I am no longer the brother of men, but the brother of all creatures and of all things!

The sun is coming up on the horizon. The breeze is dropping like the day before yesterday, but the west wind forecasted by Bernard is no more appearing than the east wind foretold by Raymond.

Until ten o'clock we floated motionless, like a wreck, then a little breath from the sea started us off again, died away, was renewed, seemed to be mocking us, irritating the sail, endlessly promising us the breeze which did not come. It was nothing, the breath from a mouth or the movement of a fan, yet it was enough to keep us from staying in the same place. Porpoises, those clowns of the sea, were playing around us, jumping out of the water with a quick spring as though they were flying, passing through the air faster than lightning, then diving and coming up farther on.

About one o'clock, as we found ourselves abreast of Agay, the breeze fell completely, and I realized that I would be sleeping at sea if I didn't man the tender to tow the yacht and to bring me into harbour in this bay.

I therefore put the two men in the dinghy, and at thirty metres off the bow they began to tow me. A raging sun fell on the water, burning the deck of the boat.

The two sailors were rowing in very slow and regular fashion, like two worn-out winches which hardly turn any more, but go on mechanically without stopping.

The Agay roads form a pretty, well-sheltered basin, closed on one side by straight, red rocks, which are overlooked by the semaphore at the top of the mountain, and extended towards the open sea by the Île d'Or, so named because of its colour, and on the other side by a line of low rocks and a tiny headland at water level, with a lighthouse to mark the entrance.

At the end there is an inn which welcomes the captains of ships seeking refuge there in bad weather, and fishermen in the summer, a station where only two trains a day stop and no one gets out, and a pretty river going deep into the Esterel as far as the valley called Malinfermet, which is as full of oleander as a gully in Africa.

From inland no road comes to this delightful bay. There is only a path leading to Saint-Raphaël, passing by the porphyry quarries of the Dramont, but no vehicle would be able to take it. So we were right in the mountains.

I decided to walk until night along the paths edged with cistus and lentiscus. Their smell of wild plants, pungent and perfumed, filled the air, mingled with the great resinous breath of the immense forest, which seemed to pant in the sun.

After an hour of walking I was surrounded by pine forest, light woodland, on a gentle slope of the mountain. The purple granite, those bones of the earth, seemed reddened by the sun, and I went on slowly, as happy as lizards must be on burning stones, when I saw at the summit of the mountain, coming towards me without seeing me, two lovers in dreamlike rapture.

It was pretty, it was charming, those two creatures with arms entwined, coming down with wandering steps, in the alternate sun and shade which coloured the slope of the hill.

She seemed to me to be very simple and elegant, with a grey travelling dress and a daring and attractive felt hat. I hardly noticed him. I simply noticed that he had an appropriate air. I had sat down behind the trunk of a pine tree to watch them pass. They didn't notice me and went on down, holding each other round the waist, without saying a word, they were so much in love.

When I could no longer see them, I felt a sadness had come into my heart. Happiness had brushed past me, a happiness I was not familiar with and which I sensed to be the best of all. And I returned towards Agay Bay, too weary now to continue my walk.

Until evening I lay on the grass at the edge of the river, and towards seven o'clock I went into the inn for dinner.

My crew had warned the landlord, who was expecting me. My place was laid in a low, white-washed room, beside another table where, already dining, face to face and gazing into each other's eyes, were my lovers of a short time ago.

I was ashamed of disturbing them, as if I were doing something improper and ugly.

They looked at me a few seconds, then began to talk very quietly.

The landlord, who had known me for a long time, took a chair near mine. He talked to me about wild boar and rabbits, about the fine weather, the mistral, an Italian captain who had slept there the other night, then, to flatter me, praised my yacht, whose black hull and big mast carrying my red and white pennant I could see through the window.

My neighbours, who had eaten very quickly, went out at once. As for me, I lingered to watch the thin crescent of the moon dusting the little bay with light. At last I saw my dinghy which was coming to the shore, dividing with its passage the pale and motionless clarity which had fallen on the water.

As I went down to embark I noticed the two lovers standing on the beach, gazing at the sea, and as I was going off to the hurried sound of the oars I was still able to make out their silhouettes on the bank, their shadows rising side by side. They were filling the bay, the night, the sky, such was the love they were emanating, spreading to the horizon, making them large and symbolic.

And when I was back on my boat, I stayed a long time sitting on deck, full of sadness without knowing why, full of regret without knowing for what, unable to make up my mind to go down finally to my cabin, as though I wanted to breathe in for longer a little of the tenderness which was spread in the air around them.

Suddenly, as one of the windows of the inn lit up, I saw their two profiles in the light. Then my solitude struck me, and in the warmth of this spring night, with the faint sound of the waves on the sand, beneath the fine crescent falling into the open sea, I felt in my heart such a desire for love that I nearly cried with distress.

Then, abruptly, I was ashamed of this weakness, and not at all wishing to admit to myself that I am a man like others are, I blamed the moonlight for having unbalanced my reason.

Besides, I have always believed the moon to exercise a mysterious influence on the human brain.

It makes poets digress, makes them delightful or ridiculous, and on the fondness of lovers it has the effect of a Ruhmkorff coil on electric currents. A man who loves normally in the sun, adores desperately beneath the moon.

A young and charming woman maintained one day, I no longer know in what connection, that moon-stroke is a thousand times more dangerous than sun-stroke. You catch it, she said, without suspecting it, as you walk on a beautiful night, and you never recover from it; you stay mad, not a raving lunatic, mad enough to lock up, but mad in a special, gentle and continuous way – you no longer think, in any way, like other men.

Certainly this evening I must have got moon-stroke, because I can feel I am unreasonable and raving, and the little crescent going down into the sea moves me, softens me and distresses me.

What then does it have that is so pleasing, this moon, an old dead star, which transports its yellow face and its sad, deathly light around the sky, so that it disturbs us so much, we people who are moved by vagabond thoughts?

Do we love it because it is dead, as the poet Haraucourt says?

Puis ce fut l'âge blond des tiédeurs et des vents.
La lune se peupla de murmures vivants:
Elle eut des mers sans fond et des fleuves sans nombre,
Des troupeaux, des cités, des pleurs, des cris joyeux,
Elle eut l'amour; elle eut ses arts, ses lois, ses dieux,
Et lentement rentra dans l'ombre. *

Do we love it because the poets, who are responsible for the eternal illusion that surrounds us in this life, have affected our vision with all the images they have seen in its light, have taught us to appreciate in a thousand ways, with our heightened sensitivity, the gentle and monochrome effect that it spreads around the world?

When it rises behind the trees, when it casts its shimmering light on a flowing river, when it falls through the branches on to sandy walks, when it climbs alone into the black and empty sky, when it drops towards the sea, spreading on the wavy and liquid surface a great train of clarity, are we not assailed by all those charming verses it inspires in great dreamers?

If we are out at night in cheerful mood, and if we see it, all round, round as a yellow eye which could be looking at us, perched just above a roof, Musset's immortal ballad begins to sing in our memory.

It is he, the mocking poet, who at once shows it to us as he sees it:

* 'Then it was the fair age of warmth and wind./ The moon was peopled with living whispers:/ It had bottomless seas and numberless rivers,/ Flocks, cities, tears and joyous cries,/ It had love; it had its arts, its laws, its gods,/ And slowly it retreated into the shade.'

C'était, dans la nuit brune,
Sur le clocher jauni,
La lune,
Comme un point sur un i.

Lune, quel esprit sombre
Promène au bout d'un fil,
Dans l'ombre,
*Ta face et ton profil?**

If, one evening when we are sad, we walk by its light on a beach at the edge of the ocean, do we not begin to recite, almost unable to help it, these two lines, so great and melancholy:

Seule au-dessus des mers, la lune, voyageant,
Laisse dans les flots noirs tomber ses pleurs d'argent.†

If we wake up in our bed, lit up by a long moonbeam coming through the window, doesn't it at once seem as though we see coming down towards us the white figure evoked by Catulle Mendès:

Elle venait, avec un lis dans chaque main,
La pente d'un rayon lui servant de chemin.‡

Walking in the country in the evening, if all at once we hear some farm dog let out its long and ominous complaint, are we not suddenly struck by the memory of that admirable piece of Leconte de Lisle's, *Les Hurleurs*?

* 'It was there, in the brown night,/ Above the yellowed bell tower,/ The moon,/ Like the dot on an i./ Moon, what sombre mind/ Pulls on the end of a line,/ In the shade,/ Your face and your profile?'
† 'Alone above the seas, the moon, travelling on,/ Lets her silver tears fall into the black waves.' Louis Bouilhet, *Les Fossiles*.
‡ 'She came, with a lily in each hand,/ The slope of a moonbeam serving as her path.'

Seule, la lune pâle, en écartant la nue,
Comme une morne lampe, oscillait tristement.

Monde muet, marqué d'un signe de colère,
Débris d'un globe mort au hasard dispersé,
Elle laissait tomber de son orbe glacé
Un reflet sépulcral sur l'océan polaire. *

On the evening of a rendezvous, you go gently along the path, an arm round the beloved's waist, pressing her hand and kissing her temple. She is a little tired, a little emotional and walks with a weary step. A bench appears, beneath the leaves, bathed in the gentle light as though by a calm wave.

Do they not leap into our mind, into our heart, like an exquisite song of love, these two charming lines:

Et réveiller, pour s'asseoir à sa place,
Le clair de lune endormi sur le banc.†

Is it possible to see the crescent outlined in fine profile, as it is this evening, in a great sky scattered with stars, without thinking of the end of Victor Hugo's masterpiece, called *Booz endormi*:

. . . et Ruth se demandait,
Immobile, ouvrant l'oeil à moitié sous ses voiles,
Quel Dieu, quel moissonneur de l'éternel été,
Avait, en s'en allant, négligemment jeté
Cette faucille d'or dans le champ des étoiles.‡

---

* 'Alone, the pale moon, coming through the cloud,/ Swung sadly like a gloomy lantern./ A dumb world, marked by a sign of anger, debris of a dead globe scattered at random,/ It let fall from its glacial orb/ A sepulchral reflection on the polar ocean.'

† 'And wake up, to sit down in its place,/ The moonlight sleeping on the bench.' Unidentified.

‡ '. . . and Ruth wondered,/ Motionless, half opening her eye under her veils,/ What God, what harvester of the eternal summer,/ Had, as he went away, carelessly thrown/ This golden sickle in the field of stars.'

And who has ever told better than Hugo of the moon who is attentive and kind to lovers?

La nuit vint; tout se tut; les flambeaux s'éteignirent;
Dans les bois assombris les sources se plaignirent;
Le rossignol, caché dans son nid ténébreux,
Chanta comme un poète et comme un amoureux.
Chacun se dispersa sous les profonds feuillages;
Les folles en riant entraînèrent les sages;
L'amante s'en alla dans l'ombre avec l'amant;
Et, troublés comme on l'est en songe, vaguement,
Ils sentaient par degrés se mêler à leur âme,
À leurs discours secrets, à leurs regards de flamme,
À leur coeur, à leurs sens, à leur molle raison,
Le clair de lune bleu qui baignait l'horizon. *

And I am reminded, too, of that admirable prayer to the moon which opens the eleventh book of the *Golden Ass* of Apuleius.

But all these songs of men are still not enough to put into our hearts the sentimental sadness that this poor star inspires in us.

We are sorry for the moon, unable to help ourselves, without knowing why, without knowing what for, and because of that we love her.

The tenderness we feel for her is also mingled with pity; we are sorry for her as though for a spinster, because we vaguely guess, in spite of the poets, that she is not dead, but a virgin.

The planets, like women, need a husband, and the poor moon, disdained by the sun, isn't she simply past marriage – braiding Saint Catherine's tresses, as we say here below?

* 'Night came; all was silence; the torches burned down,/ In the darkened woods came the plaint of springs;/ The nightingale, hidden in its shadowed nest,/ Sang like a poet and like a lover./ Each one scattered under the deep foliage,/ The frivolous, laughing, led away the sage;/ Lover went with lover in the shade;/ And, disturbed vaguely as one is in dreams,/ They felt little by little mingled in their soul,/ In their secret talks, in their burning looks,/ In their heart, their senses, in their feeble reason,/ The blue moonlight bathing the horizon.'

That is why it fills us, with its timid clarity, with unrealizable hopes and inaccessible desires. Everything we obscurely and vainly expect on this earth lifts our heart like impotent and mysterious sap beneath the pale rays of the moon. Eyes raised to it, we are a-quiver with impossible dreams and thirsty for inexpressible affection.

The slim crescent, a golden thread, was now dipping its sharp point into the water, and it gently, slowly plunged as far as the other point, so fine that I didn't see it disappear.

I lifted my gaze to the inn. The lighted window had just closed. Deep distress crushed me, and I went down to my cabin.

I was scarcely in bed when I felt that I would not sleep, and I stayed on my back, eyes closed, thoughts active, nerves tense. Not a movement, not a sound, far or near; only the breathing of the two sailors came through the thin wooden bulkhead.

Suddenly something squeaked. What? I don't know, a block in the rigging no doubt, but the sound of this noise, so gentle, so painful, so plaintive, made my flesh creep. Then nothing, infinite silence from the land to the stars; nothing, not a whisper, not a ripple in the water nor a vibration in the yacht, nothing. Then suddenly the unidentifiable and so feeble whining began again. It seemed to me, as I heard it, that a broken blade was sawing at my heart. How certain noises, certain notes, certain voices do tear us apart, are able to cast into the soul in one second as much pain, fear and anguish as it can hold! I was listening expectantly, and I heard it again, that noise which seemed to come out of myself, torn from my nerves, or rather which sounded inside me, like a deep, intimate and desolate call. Yes, it was a cruel voice, a voice that was known, expected and that made me despair. This weak and outlandish sound passed over me like the spreading of horror and madness, as it immediately had the power to awaken the terrible distress that is always sleeping at the bottom of the heart of everyone alive. What was it? It was the voice that cries unendingly in our mind, and reproaches us in a continuous fashion, obscurely and painfully, torturing, harassing, unknown, unappeasable, unforgettable and ferocious, that blames us for everything we have done and simultaneously for everything we have not done, the voice of vague remorse, of regret with no going back, of days gone, of women encountered who might perhaps have loved us, of things vanished, of vain joy, of dead hope; the voice of that which passes, flees, deceives, disappears, of that which we have not achieved, will never reach, the thin little voice that cries out at an aborted life, of the uselessness of effort, of the impotence of the mind and the weakness of the flesh.

It told me in this brief whisper, always starting up again after the sombre silence of the dead of night, it told me about everything I could have loved, everything that, in confusion, I had wanted, expected, dreamed about, everything I could have wished to see, understand, know, taste, everything that my insatiable and poor and feeble mind had skimmed over with vain hope, everything towards which it had tried to soar, without being able to break the chain of ignorance that held it back.

Ah! I have coveted everything and enjoyed nothing. I would have needed the vitality of an entire race, the varied intelligences spread among all beings, every faculty, every power, and a thousand existences in reserve, since I have in me all the appetites and all the curiosities, and I am reduced to watching everything and holding nothing.

Then why this distress at living, when most men only feel its satisfaction? Why this unknown torture gnawing at me? Why not experience the reality of pleasure, of expectation, of enjoyment?

It is because I have in me this second vision, which is at the same time the strength and the entire unhappiness of writers. I write because I understand and am tolerant towards everything there is, because I know too much about it and especially because, without being able to experience it, I see it in myself, in the mirror of my mind.

We should not be envied, but pitied, for this is how a man

of letters differs from his fellow men.

In him, no simple feeling exists any more. Everything he sees, his joys, his pleasures, his pain, his despair instantly become subjects for observation. He analyses in spite of everything, in spite of himself, endlessly, hearts, faces, gestures, intonations. As soon as he has seen, whatever he has seen, he must know the reason why! He hasn't an impulse, a cry or a kiss which are straightforward, he has not one of those instantaneous actions which one does because one has to, without thinking, without knowing, without understanding, without going over it afterwards.

If he suffers, he makes a note of his pain and files it in his memory; he says to himself as he comes back from the cemetery where he has left him or her he most loved in the world, 'It's odd what I felt; it was like a painful state of heightened emotion, etc.' And then he remembers all the details, the false faces and a thousand little insignificant things, the observations of an artist, the sign of the cross made by an old lady who held a child by the hand, a ray of light in a window, a dog which crossed the funeral procession, the effect of the hearse under the great yews in the cemetery, the head of the undertaker's man and the contraction of the features, the effort of the four men who let the bier down into the grave, in fact a thousand things which a good man suffering with all his heart, with all his soul, with all his strength, would never have noticed.

He has seen everything, noted everything, retained everything, unable to help it because above all he is a man of letters and his mind is formed in such a way that to him the repercussions are much sharper, more natural so to speak, than the first knock, the echo more resounding than the original sound.

He seems to have two minds, one that notes, explains and comments on every feeling of its neighbour, of the natural mind, the one all men have, and he lives condemned forever, at every moment, to be a reflection of himself and a reflection of others, condemned to watch himself feel, act, love, think, suffer, and never to suffer, think, love, feel like everyone else does, kindly, truly, simply, without self-analysis after each joy and after each sob.

If he is talking, his words sometimes seem malicious, simply because his thoughts are penetrating, and he reveals all the hidden motivations in the feelings and actions of others.

If he is writing, he cannot refrain from throwing into his books everything he has seen, everything he has understood, everything he knows, and he does so with no exception for relatives and friends, laying bare with cruel impartiality the hearts of those he loves or has loved, even exaggerating to increase the effect, solely concerned with his work and not at all with his attachments.

And if he loves, if he loves a woman, he dissects her like a corpse in a hospital. Everything she says and does is instantly weighed in his delicate scales of observation and classified according to its documentary value. Should she throw herself round his neck with a thoughtless impulse, he will judge the movement according to its appropriateness, its correctness, its dramatic power, and will tacitly condemn it if he feels it to be false or badly done.

Actor and spectator of himself and of others, he is never only an actor like good people who live without artifice. Everything, all around him, becomes like glass, hearts, deeds and secret intentions, and he suffers from a strange ailment, a sort of dividing of the mind, which makes him into a frighteningly impassioned, calculating, complex creature, who is exhausting for himself.

His special, unhealthy sensibility also gives him an acute sensitivity, which turns almost every feeling into pain.

I can remember black days when my heart was so torn by things seen for a second that the memory of these sights remained with me like wounds.

One morning in the avenue de l'Opéra in the middle of a moving and happy crowd elated by the May sunshine, I suddenly saw an indescribable creature passing by, an old lady bent in two, wearing tatters that had once been dresses, on her head a black straw hat, quite bare of its original trimmings, ribbons and flowers long since gone. And she was moving, dragging her feet with such difficulty that I felt in my heart as much as she did, more than she did, the pain of every step. Two sticks held her up. She passed by without seeing anyone, indifferent to everything, the noise, the people, the carriages, the sun! Where was she going? To what hovel? She was carrying something in a paper which hung at the end of a string. What? Bread? Yes, probably. No one, no neighbour having been able or willing to do this shopping for her, she had gone herself on this terrible journey from her garret to the baker. Two hours at least there and back. And what a painful journey! What a way of the cross more frightful than Christ's!

I raised my eyes to the roofs of the huge houses. She was going up there! When would she get there? How many breathless stops on the steps, on the little black and winding staircase?

Everyone turned to look at her. They murmured, 'Poor woman!', then passed by. Her skirt, her rag of a skirt dragged on the pavement, hardly attached to the remains of her body. And there were thoughts in there. Thoughts? No, but incessant, harassing, horrifying suffering. Oh! the misery of the old with no bread, the old with no hope, no children, no money, with nothing but death in front of them, do we think about it? Do we think of the hungry old people in their garrets? Do we think about the tears in those dull eyes, which were once joyful, excited and shining?

Another time it was raining, I was going hunting by myself on the Norman plain, across the great ploughed fields of slippery mud which softened and slid under my feet. From time to time a startled partridge, hidden against a clod of earth, would take clumsy flight in the pouring rain. My gunshot was like the crack of a whip, hardly sounding, muted by the sheets of water falling from the sky, and the grey bird dropped with blood on its feathers.

I felt sad enough to cry, to cry like the clouds which were crying on the world and on me, soaked to the heart with sadness, so crushed with weariness that my legs, sticky with clay, would move no more; I was going to go back when I saw the doctor's gig in the middle of the fields, following a path across.

It passed by, the low black carriage, covered with its round hood and drawn by its brown horse, like an augur of death wandering about the countryside on this sinister day. Suddenly it stopped; the doctor's head appeared and he cried 'Hey!'

I went towards him. He said to me, 'Will you help me treat a case of diphtheria? I am alone and she needs to be held while I remove the false membrane from her throat.'

'I'll come with you,' I replied. And I got into his gig.

This is what he told me.

Fever, the dreadful fever that chokes wretched men, had got into the Martinets' farm, poor people. Father and son had died at the beginning of the week. Mother and daughter were now going that way too.

A neighbour who was looking after them, suddenly feeling unwell, had fled only the day before, leaving the door open and the two sick women abandoned on their mean straw beds, with nothing to drink, alone, breathing hoarsely, suffocating, dying, alone for the last twenty-four hours.

The doctor had already been to clear the mother's throat and give her something to drink, but the child, terrified by pain and by the torment of suffocating, had buried and hidden her head in the straw mattress and would not let herself be touched.

Accustomed to such distress, the doctor said in sad and resigned tones, 'All the same I can't spend the whole day with my patients. Good Lord, these break your heart. When you think that they were twenty-four hours with nothing to drink. The wind was driving the rain right up to their beds. All the hens were sheltering in the fireplace.'

We were arriving at the farm. He tied his horse to the branch of an apple tree in front of the door, and we went in.

A heavy smell of illness and damp, of fever and mould, of hospital and cellar, caught at our throats. It was cold, the coldness of a marsh, in this house without fire and without life, grey and sinister. The clock had stopped; the rain was coming down the big chimney into the fireplace, where the hens had scattered the ashes, and you could hear from a dark corner a noise like quick, hoarse bellows. It was the child's breathing.

The mother, stretched out in a sort of big wooden box, the bed they have in the country, hidden by old blankets and old clothes, seemed peaceful. She turned her head towards us a little.

The doctor asked her, 'Do you have a candle?'

She replied in a low voice, exhausted, 'In the sideboard.'

He took the light and led me to the back of the room, to the little girl's small bed.

She was panting, her cheeks hollow, her eyes glittering, her hair tangled, a frightening sight. In her thin, tense neck deep hollows were forming with every aspiration. Stretched out on her back she was gripping the rags that covered her with both hands; as soon as she saw us she turned on her face to hide in the bed.

I took her by the shoulders, and the doctor, forcing her to expose her throat, tore a big, whitish skin from it, which seemed to me as dry as leather.

Her breathing improved at once, and she drank a little. The mother, raised on an elbow, looked at us. She stammered, "'Tis done?'

'Yes, it is done.'

'Does we stay by ourselves?'

Fear, terrible fear, made her voice tremble, fear of this isolation, of being abandoned, of the darkness and of the death she felt to be so close.

I replied, 'No, my good woman; I'll wait until the doctor has sent the nurse,' and turning to the doctor, 'Send her Mother Mauduit. I will pay her.'

'Ideal. I'll send her straight away.' He shook my hand and left; I heard his gig going off along the wet road.

I was alone with the two dying women.

My dog Paf was lying down in front of the black fireplace, and he made me think that some fire would do us all good. So I went out again to look for wood and straw, and soon a big blaze lit up the far end of the room and the bed with the little girl, who was beginning to pant again.

I sat down, stretching my legs towards the fire. The rain was beating against the windows; the wind was shaking the roof; I could hear the short, hard, whistling respiration of the two women, and the breathing of my dog, who was whimpering with pleasure, stretched out in front of the bright hearth.

Life, life! What is it? These two poor people who have always slept on straw, eaten black bread, worked like beasts, suffered all the miseries on earth, were going to die. What had they done? The father was dead, the son was dead. Yet these poor things seemed to be good folk who were well liked and respected, simple and honest people.

I was looking at my steaming boots and my sleeping dog,

when I suddenly felt a sensual and shameful joy at the comparison of my lot with that of these slaves!

The little girl began to rale and suddenly this raucous breathing became unbearable; it tore me apart, like something sharp being driven into my heart.

I went towards her. 'Would you like a drink?' I said.

She nodded her head, and I poured a little water into her mouth, but it did not go down.

The mother, who was calmer, had turned to look at her child, and then suddenly I felt a shiver of fear, a sinister fear which slipped under my skin like the touch of an invisible monster. Where was I? I no longer knew. Was I dreaming? What nightmare had gripped me?

Was it true that things like this happened, that you could die like this? And I looked into the dark corners of the cottage as if I had expected to see, crouched in a dark corner, a hideous, unmentionable, terrifying shape, who stalks men's lives and kills, consumes, crushes, strangles them; one who loves red blood, eyes lit up with fever, wrinkles and withering flesh, white hair and decomposition.

The fire was going out. I threw on some wood and warmed my back against it, so chilled were my loins. At least I myself could hope to die in a comfortable bedroom, with doctors round my bed, and medicines on the tables.

And these women had stayed alone for twenty-four hours in this fireless shack, choking on the straw!

Suddenly I heard the trotting of a horse and the sound of wheels, and the nurse came in, serene, happy to have found work, with no surprise at this misery. I left her some money and fled with my dog; I fled like a malefactor, running in the rain, thinking I could still hear the whistling of the two throats, running towards my warm house where my servants waited for me as they prepared a good dinner.

But I will never forget that, and so many other things as well, which make me hate the world.

How I would like sometimes not to think any more, not to feel any more; I would like to live like a brute, in a bright, hot country, in a golden country, with no crude and harsh greenness, in one of those Oriental countries where going to sleep has no sadness, waking no distress, where action is carefree, where love has no anguish, where existence is scarcely felt.

I would live in a vast, square house, like a huge box shining in the sun.

From the terrace the sea can be seen, where those white sails, like pointed wings, of Greek or Muslim boats are passing by. The outside walls have almost no openings. A big garden, where the air is heavy under the parasol of the palm trees, forms the centre of this eastern house. A jet of water goes up under the trees and turns to spray as it falls into a large marble basin, whose base is powdered with gold dust. I would bathe in it at any moment, between two pipes, two dreams or two kisses.

I would have black and beautiful slaves, draped in light materials and running quickly, barefoot, on soundless carpets.

My walls would be soft and resilient as the breasts of women and on my divans encircling each room, every shape of cushion would allow me to lie in all the postures it is possible to adopt.

Then, when I would have had enough of pleasurable rest, enough of enjoying immobility and my endless dream, enough of the calm pleasure of being at ease, I would have brought to my door a white or black horse, supple as a gazelle.

I would go off on its back, drinking in the air that whips and intoxicates, the whistling air of furious gallops, and I would speed like an arrow over this coloured earth which enraptures the eye, the sight of which is as delectable as wine.

In the calm of the evening I would go, in a mad race, towards the wide horizon which the setting sun tints with rose. Everything becomes rose-coloured there, at dusk, the burnt mountains, the sand, the clothes of the Arabs, the dromedaries, the horses and the tents.

The pink flamingos take flight from the marshes against a rose-coloured sky; and I would utter delirious cries, drowned in the infinite rosiness of the world.

I would no longer see men dressed in black all along the pavements, deafened by the hard noise of the cabs on the *pavé*, sitting on uncomfortable chairs, drinking absinthe and talking business.

I would know nothing about stock exchange rates, political events, government changes, all the useless idiocy with which we waste our short and deceptive existence. Why all these efforts, these miseries, these struggles? I would rest, sheltered from the wind, in my light and sumptous abode.

I would have four or five wives in discreet and soundless apartments, five wives from the five corners of the world, who would bring me a taste of the feminine beauty flourishing in every race.

The winged dream was floating before my closed eyes, in my mind which was becoming calmer, when I heard that my men were waking up, that they were lighting their lantern and starting to work at some long and silent task.

I called out to them, 'What are you doing then?'

Raymond replied in a hesitant voice, 'We are getting a long-line ready because we thought you might like to fish, sir, if it is fine at dawn.'

In fact Agay is the meeting place, in summer, of all the fishermen on the coast. They come there with their families, sleeping at the inn or on their boats, and they eat *bouillabaisse* by the sea, in the shade of the pines, whose hot resin spits in the sun.

I asked, 'What time is it?'

'Three o'clock, sir.'

So without getting up, stretching out my arm, I opened the door that separated my cabin from the crew's quarters.

The two men were in the sort of low recess which the mast passes through in order to embed itself in the keel, in that recess so full of strange and weird objects that it seems like a bandit's hideout, where instruments of every kind can be seen hanging in orderly fashion all along the bulkheads, saws, axes, marlin-spikes, tackle and saucepans, then, on the ground between the two bunks, a bucket, a stove, a barrel, whose copper hoops shine in the direct light of the lantern hanging above the anchor bitts, beside the chain locker. My crew were working at baiting the innumerable hooks hanging along the line.

'What time do I have to get up?' I said to them.

'Straight away, sir.'

Half an hour later we were all three getting into the dinghy and we were leaving the *Bel-Ami* to go and spread our net at the foot of the Dramont, near the Île d'Or.

Then, when our long-line, two or three hundred metres long, had dropped down to the sea bed, we baited three small bottom lines and, having anchored the dinghy with a stone on the end of a rope, we began to fish.

It was already daylight and I could see the coastline of Saint-Raphaël very well, close to the mouth of the Argens river, and the dark Maures mountains, running as far as Cap Camarat over there, out at sea, beyond Saint-Tropez Bay.

Of all the coast of the South of France, it is the place I love best. I love it as though I had been born there, as though I had grown up there, because it is wild and colourful, and not yet poisoned by the Parisians, the English, the Americans, the men of the world and the *rastaquouères*.*

Suddenly the line I was holding in my hand trembled, I jumped, then nothing, then a light tug tightened the cord rolled round my fingers, then another stronger one moved my hand and, heart beating, I began to pull the line, gently, eagerly, looking deeply into the blue and transparent water, and soon I saw in the shadow of the boat a white flash which was moving in rapid curves.

Seen like that, this fish seemed to me to be enormous – the size of a sardine when it was on board.

Then I had more of them, blue ones, red ones, green and yellow ones, shining, silvery, striped, golden, with rainbow spots, patches, these pretty rock fish of the Mediterranean, so variegated, so brightly coloured, which seem to be painted as a feast for the eyes, then the *rascasses* with barbed spines, and Moray eels, those hideous monsters.

Nothing is more entertaining than pulling in a long-line. What is going to come out of this sea? What surprise, what joy or what disillusion at every hook that comes out of the water! What emotion as from far off we catch sight of a big creature which is struggling as it slowly climbs towards us!

* Someone from South America or a southern country with a vulgar and obvious taste for luxury, appearing to be rich, but of highly dubious authenticity. A very expressive neologism in the 1880s, the word seems to have been coined by the journalist Fervacques in the 1870s and became widely used.

At ten o'clock we were back on board the yacht and the two beaming men informed me that our catch weighed eleven kilos.

But I was going to pay for my sleepless night! Migraine, that awful affliction, migraine, which tortures as no other persecution could do, which crushes your head, drives you crazy, confuses ideas and drives memory away like dust in the wind, migraine had seized me, and I had to lie down on my bunk, a bottle of ether at my nose.

After a few minutes I thought I could hear a vague murmuring which soon became a kind of buzzing, and it seemed to me that all the inside of my body was becoming light, light as air, that it was vaporizing.

Then came a kind of lethargy of spirit, a sleepy well-being in spite of the pain, which persisted, but which, however, was ceasing to be dreadful. It was one of those aches you can put up with, and no longer one of the frightful torments against which the whole suffering body protests.

Soon the strange and delightful sensation of emptiness I had in my chest extended, reached my limbs, which became light in their turn, light as if the bones and the flesh might have melted away and only the skin was left, the skin being needed to make me aware of the pleasure of being alive, of being stretched out in this comfort. Then I noticed that my head was no longer hurting. The pain too had gone off and melted away, evaporated. And I heard voices, four voices, two dialogues, without understanding any of the words. Sometimes it was only indistinct sounds, sometimes a word got through to me. But I realized that it was simply an accentuation of the buzzing in my ears. I was not asleep, I was awake; I was understanding, I was feeling, I was reasoning with an accuracy, a depth, a power which were extraordinary, and with a pleasure, a strange rapture that was the result of this intensification of my mental faculties.

It was not a dream like that of hashish, it was not the rather sickly visions of opium; it was marvellously keen reasoning, a new way of seeing, judging, appreciating things and life, with the certainty, the complete awareness, that this way was the right one.

And the old image from the Scriptures suddenly came into my mind. It seemed to me that I had tasted of the Tree of Knowledge, that all the mysteries had been unveiled, so much did I find myself under the sway of a new, strange, irrefutable logic. And arguments, reasonings, proofs came to me in hordes, immediately reversed by a stronger proof, reasoning, argument. My head became a battlefield of ideas. I was a superior being, armed with invincible intelligence, and I experienced marvellous pleasure at the recognition of my power....

That went on for so long, so long. I was still breathing from my open bottle of ether. Suddenly I noticed it was empty, and the pain began again.

For ten hours I had to endure this torture for which there are no remedies, then I slept, and the next day, alert as though after a convalescence, having written these few pages, I left for Saint-Raphaël.

We had delightful weather for getting here, a light breeze from the west which brought us in six tacks. After passing the Dramont I could see the villas of Saint-Raphaël hidden in the pine trees, in the little, thin pines which are exhausted the whole year long by the incessant Fréjus wind. Then I passed between the Lions, pretty red rocks that seem to guard the town, and I entered the port with its sandy beach, which makes you stand off fifty metres from the quay, and I went ashore.

There were a lot of people assembled in front of the church. Someone was getting married inside. A priest was authorizing, in Latin, with the gravity of a Pope, the comic, solemn and animal act that so excites men, makes them suffer so much, laugh so much and cry so much. The families, according to custom, had invited all their relatives and all their friends to this funeral service for the innocence of a young girl, to this pious and unseemly spectacle of ecclesiastical advice taking precedence over that of her mother and of a public blessing being given to what is usually so carefully and modestly veiled.

And the whole neighbourhood, full of licentious ideas, moved by the leering and avid curiosity which draws crowds to this sight, had come there to see how the bridal couple looked. I went among the crowd and I looked at it.

God, how ugly men are! For the hundredth time at least I noticed in the middle of this celebration that, of all races, the human race is the most hideous. And the smell of people was drifting about, a stale and nauseating smell of unclean flesh, of greasy hair and of garlic, that scent of garlic which the people of the Midi spread all round them, from their mouths, from their noses and from their skin, just as roses diffuse their perfume.

It is true that every day men are as ugly and every day they smell as bad, but our eyes, which are used to seeing them, our noses, which are used to smelling them, only notice their hideousness and their emissions when we have been deprived for a while of the sight and the stench.

Man is hideous! To create a picture gallery so grotesque it would make a corpse laugh, it would be sufficient to take the first ten people who pass by, to line them up and photograph them with their unequal sizes, their legs too long or too short, their bodies too fat or too thin, their faces red or pale, bearded or smooth, their smiling or serious air.

Once, when the world was young, savage man, strong and naked, was most certainly as beautiful as the horse, the deer or the lion. The working of his muscles, the free life, the constant use of his vigour and his agility, preserved in him the grace of movement which is the primary requirement of beauty, and the elegance of form only given by physical exercise. Later on, races of artistic temperament, much taken with sculptural beauty, learned how to maintain this grace and elegance in men of intelligence by the device of gymnastics. Care of the body, games using strength and suppleness, icy water and steam made the Greeks real models of human beauty, and they left us their statues as a lesson, to show what the bodies of these great artists were like.

But today, O Apollo, look at the human race moving about on holidays! The children, pot-bellied from the cradle, deformed by premature study, stupefied by an education that wears out their body at fifteen while bending their mind before it is mature, arrive at adolescence with limbs badly grown, badly jointed, which never keep their normal proportions.

Then look at the street, at the people going by with their dirty clothes! As for the country people! Good Lord! Go and look at the labourer in the fields, the man of the soil, knobbly, long as a pole, always crooked, bent, more frightful than the barbarian types you see in an anthropological museum.

And think of the beauty of form, if not of face, of Negroes, these men of bronze, tall and supple, and how elegant in shape and face are the Arabs!

Besides, for yet another reason I have a horror of crowds.

I cannot enter a theatre nor be present at a public festival. I immediately feel an extraordinary, intolerable unease, a terrible nervous irritation as though I were fighting with all my strength against an irresistible and mysterious influence, and indeed I am fighting against the mood of the crowd which is trying to take me over.

How many times I have noticed that understanding becomes greater and more elevated once you live alone, that it is lessened and abased on mixing once more with other men. Relationships, accepted ideas, everything that is said, everything you are forced to listen to, hear and answer have their effect on thought. An ebb and flow of ideas goes from head to head, from house to house, from street to street, from town to town, from people to people, and a level becomes established, an average of comprehension for every sizeable grouping of individuals.

Qualities of intellectual initiative, of free choice, of balanced reflection, and even of shrewdness, which are in every man in isolation, generally disappear as soon as that man mixes with a large number of other men.

Take this passage from a letter from Lord Chesterfield to his son (1751), which shows with rare humility this sudden elimination of the active qualities of the mind in any large meeting:

Lord Macclesfield, who has had the greater part in the preparation of the bill and who is one of the greatest mathematicians and astronomers in England, then spoke with profound understanding of the question, and with all the clarity which such a complicated matter could require. But since his words, his phrases and his speech were

76

worth far less than mine, I was given preference unanimously, most unjustly, I confess.

It will always be so. Every assembly is a *crowd*; whatever the individuals who compose it, you must never attribute to a crowd the language of pure reason. You must only address its passions, its feelings and its obvious interests.

A group of individuals no longer has the faculty of understanding, etc.

This penetrating observation of Lord Chesterfield's, an observation, moreover, that was often made and noted with interest by the philosophers of the scientific school, constitutes one of the most convincing arguments against representative government.

The same phenomenon, a surprising phenomenon, comes about each time a large number of men are gathered together. All of these people, side by side, separate, different in mind, intelligence, passion, prejudice, education, belief, all of a sudden, due only to their presence together, produce a distinct creature with a mind of its own, a new and communal way of thinking which is the result, defying analysis, of the average of the individual opinions.

It is a crowd, and this crowd is someone, a vast collective individual, as distinct from another crowd as one man is distinct from another man.

A popular saying has it that 'a crowd does not reason'. Now why does a crowd have no ability to reason, when every individual in the crowd can reason? Why does a crowd spontaneously do what not one of the units in that crowd would have done? Why does a crowd have irresistible impulses, a savage will, the ability to be stupidly carried away which nothing can stop and, when thoughtlessly carried away, why does it commit acts that not one of the individuals who compose it would do?

An unknown person cries out, and see how a kind of frenzy comes over everyone, and all, on the same impulse, which no one tries to resist, are carried away by a single thought which instantly becomes common to them all. In spite of differences in their opinions, acts, beliefs and principles, they will fall upon a man, will slaughter him, drown him without justification, almost without excuse, while each of them, had he been alone, would have rushed, at the risk of his life, to save the one he kills.

That evening at home each one will ask himself what rage or madness gripped him, threw him abruptly out of character and against his nature, how he was able to give in to this wild impulse.

It is because he had stopped being a man to be part of a crowd. His individual will had been merged with the common will just as a drop of water merges with a river.

His personality had disappeared, becoming a minute part of a vast and peculiar personality, that of the crowd. The panic that grips an army and the hurricanes of opinion that carry away an entire people, and the insanity of a *danse macabre*, are they not further striking examples of this same phenomenon?

After all, it is no more surprising to see individuals uniting to form a whole than to see molecules coming together to form a body.

It is this mysterious process which must explain the mood that is so specific to theatres, and the very bizarre variations in opinion in the audience for a dress rehearsal compared with the audience on a first night, and a first-night audience with the performances that follow, and the shifting of the effect from one evening to another, and the errors of judgement that condemn works like *Carmen*, which are destined later to be an immense success.

Furthermore, what I have said about crowds must apply to the whole of society, and he who would wish to keep complete integrity of thought, a proudly independent judgement, to see life, humanity and the universe as a free observer, beyond all prejudice, all preconceived ideas and all religions, in other words above any fear, should completely avoid what are called social relations, because universal stupidity is so contagious that he cannot encounter his fellow men, see and hear them without being undermined on all sides, in spite of himself, by their convictions, their ideas, their superstitions, their traditions, their prejudices which cause their customs, their rules and their astonishing morality of hypocrisy and cowardice to rebound on to him.

Those who try to resist these incessant and belittling influences struggle in vain amidst minute, inescapable, innumerable and almost imperceptible bonds. Then, becoming tired, one ceases to struggle.

There was a movement among the spectators, the bridal pair were going to come out. Suddenly, I did the same as everyone else, I rose on tiptoe to see, and I did want to see – a stupid, low, repellent desire, a desire of the masses. The curiosity of my neighbours had come over me like drunkenness; I was part of this crowd.

To occupy the rest of my day, I decided to go on a trip in the dinghy up the Argens. This river, enchanting and almost unknown, separates the plain of Fréjus from the wild Maures mountains.

I took Raymond, who rowed me, skirting a large, flat beach, as far as the mouth, which we found impassable and partly silted up. A single canal communicated with the sea, but it was so rapid, so full of spray, of movement and of whirlpools that we were not able to attempt it.

So we had to drag the dinghy ashore and carry it in our arms over the dunes as far as the wonderful lake-like expanse which the Argens forms at this spot.

In the middle of a marshy and green landscape, that strong green of trees growing in the water, the river goes deep between two banks so covered with greenery, with tall and impenetrable leaves, that you hardly notice the neighbouring mountains; it plunges in, always turning, always keeping its air of peaceful lake, without ever letting it be seen or guessed that it is continuing its way across this calm countryside, deserted and magnificent.

Just like those flat plains in the north, where springs ooze under your feet, flowing and reviving the earth like blood, the clear and icy blood of the soil, you rediscover here the strange sensation of abundant life which floats over wet regions.

Birds with big drooping feet fly up from the reeds, stretching their pointed beaks to the sky; others, large and heavy, pass from one bank to the other in ponderous flight; still others,

79

smaller and quicker, skim over the river, thrown like a stone that ricochets. The turtle doves, uncountable, coo in the treetops or wheel round, go from one tree to another, seem to be exchanging loving visits. You can feel that everywhere all around this deep water, in all this plain up to the foot of the mountains, there is still more water, the deceptive, sleepy and alive water of the marshes, the big clear expanses that mirror the sky, in which clouds glide and from which emerge scattered groups of curious rushes, the clear and fecund water where life decomposes, where death ferments, the water that nourishes fevers and miasmas, which is at the same time a sap and a poison, and is spread, pretty and attractive, over mysterious putrefactions. The air breathed in is delicious, enervating and dangerous. On these banks which separate the big tranquil pools, in all the thick plants, swarms, jumps, creeps and crawls the viscous and repellent race of animals who have icy blood. I love these cold and shy creatures which are feared and avoided; to me they have something sacred about them.

When the sun is setting, the marsh infatuates and enraptures me. Having been all day a great silent pool, drowsy under the sun, it becomes, at the moment of dusk, a fairylike and supernatural place. Into its calm and endless mirror clouds fall, golden clouds, clouds like blood, clouds of fire; they fall in, dip in, drown, languish there. They are up there, in the immense sky, and they are below, under us, so close yet elusive, in this thin puddle of water which is pierced as though with hairs by pointed grasses.

All the colour the world has, charming, exhilarating and varied, seems delightfully finite, marvellously striking, endlessly shaded, all around a waterlily leaf. All the reds, all the pinks, all the yellows, all the blues, all the greens, all the violets are there, in a little water which shows us all the sky, all of space, all dreams, where flights of birds pass by. And then there is something else besides, I don't know what, in the marshes, at sunset. I feel it like the confused revelation of an unknowable mystery, the original breath of primitive life, perhaps a bubble of gas which came out of a marsh as the day died.

We left Saint-Raphaël this morning at about eight o'clock, with a strong north-west breeze.

The sea, without waves in the bay, was white with foam, white like a sheet of soapsuds, for the wind, the terrible Fréjus wind that blows almost every morning, seemed to fall upon it to tear off the skin, which it lifted and rolled into little billows of froth, scattered, then at once formed again.

As the people in the port had declared that this squall would drop at around eleven o'clock, we made up our minds to start out with three reefs and the small jib.

The dinghy was brought on deck and stowed at the foot of the mast, and the *Bel-Ami* seemed to take flight as soon as she left the jetty. Even though she was carrying almost no sail, I had never felt her run like that. You could almost say she was not touching the water, and you would hardly suspect that at the bottom of her wide keel, two metres deep, she was carrying an eighteen-hundred-kilogram piece of lead, not to mention two thousand kilos of ballast in the hold and all the gear we had on board, anchors, chains, mooring ropes and fittings.

I had very quickly crossed the bay, at the end of which the

Argens pours out, and once I was in the lee of the coast the breeze dropped almost completely. It is there that this wild, sombre and magnificent region begins, still called the land of the Moors. It is a long range of mountains and only the coastline has any development of more than a hundred kilometres.

Saint-Tropez, at the entrance to the lovely bay once called Grimaud Bay, is the capital of this little Saracen kingdom, in which almost all the villages, built at the top of peaks to keep them safe from attacks, are still full of Moorish houses, with their archways, their narrow windows and their interior courtyards where tall palm trees grow, and now they are over the rooftops.

If you go on foot right into the unknown valleys of this strange mountain mass, you discover an incredibly wild country, with no roads, no paths, even with no tracks, no hamlets, no houses. From time to time, after seven or eight hours of walking, you catch sight of a hut, often abandoned, and sometimes lived in by a poor family of charcoal burners. The Maures mountains apparently have a quite exceptional geological system, an incomparable flora, the most varied in Europe it is said, and immense forests of pines, cork oaks and chestnut trees.

Three years ago now, I made an excursion into the heart of the country, to the ruins of the Verne Carthusian monastery, of which I have an indelible memory. If it is fine tomorrow, I will go back there.

A new road follows the sea, going from Saint-Raphaël to Saint-Tropez. All along this magnificent avenue, opened up through the forest on to an incomparable coastline, they are trying to create resorts for winter visitors.

The first one planned is Saint-Aygulf. This one has something unusual about it. In the middle of pine woods which come down to the sea, wide paths open up in every direction. There is not a single house, nothing but the plan of the streets running through the trees. There are squares, crossroads, boulevards. Their names are even inscribed on metal plaques: Boulevard Ruysdael, Boulevard Rubens, Boulevard Van Dyck, Boulevard Claude Lorrain. One asks why all these artists? Ah!

Why? It is because the development company said, like God himself before he lit up the sun, 'Let there be an artistic resort!'

The development company! The rest of the world does not realize all that these words mean in terms of hopes, dangers, of money won and lost on the Mediterranean! The development company! That enigmatic, inevitable, significant, deceptive term!

However, the company appears to be achieving its hopes in this spot for it already has buyers, and good ones, among artistic people. Here and there you read, 'Plot bought by Monsieur Carolus-Duran; Monsieur Clairin's plot; Mademoiselle Croizette's plot, etc.' Yet . . . who knows? The Mediterranean companies are not in luck.

Nothing is more comic than this furious speculation which ends in spectacular bankruptcies. Anyone who had made ten thousand francs on a field spends ten million on land at twenty sous the square metre, to sell it on again at twenty francs a metre. The boulevards are marked, the water is brought, they make a start on the gas, and they wait for the buyers. The buyers don't come, but disaster does.

I could see, far in front of me, the towers and the buoys that mark the breakers on the two shores at the mouth of Saint-Tropez Bay. The first tower is called the Sardinaux tower and marks a real bank of rocks at water level, some of which are showing their brown tops, and the second was named the *Sèche à l'huile* beacon.

Now we were arriving at the entrance to the bay, which goes on into the distance between the two banks of mountains and forests as far as the village of Grimaud, built on the top of a hill right at the end. The ancient château of the Grimaldis, a tall ruin which dominates the village, was appearing in the distance through the mist like something out of a fairy story.

There was no more wind. The bay was like an immense, calm lake which we entered gently, using the dying breaths of the morning's squall. To the right of the passage Sainte-Maxime, a little white port, was reflected in the water, where the mirror image of the houses was reproduced, head down, as clearly as on the bank. Opposite, Saint-Tropez appeared, protected by an old fort.

At eleven o'clock the *Bel-Ami* was mooring at the quay, next to the little steamer which is the ferry to Saint-Raphaël. In fact this *Sea-Lion*, an old cruising yacht, together with an old diligence that takes the mail and leaves at night by the only road that crosses these mountains, is all there is to keep the inhabitants of this isolated little port in touch with the rest of the world.

It is one of those simple and charming daughters of the sea, one of those good, modest little towns, pushed into the water like a sea-shell, fed on fish and sea air and producing sailors. At the port rises up the bronze statue of the Bailli de Suffren.*

You can smell fishing and burning tar, salting brine and the hulls of the boats. You can see sardine scales shining like pearls on the *pavé* of the streets, and all along the walls of the port the limping, crippled population of old sailors warming themselves in the sun on stone benches. From time to time they tell of past voyages, and of those they used to know, the grandfathers of the children running about nearby. Their hands and their faces are wrinkled, darkened, dried, tanned by the wind, the work, the spray, the heat of the equator and the cold of the northern seas, for as they roamed over the oceans they saw the top and the bottom of the world, and the far side of all the lands and all the latitudes. In front of them, leaning on a stick, a former deep-sea captain passes by, who commanded the *Trois-Sœurs*, or the *Deux-Amis*, or the *Marie-Louise*, or the *Jeune-Clémentine*. All of them greet him, like soldiers responding to a bugle call, with a litany of 'Good morning, Captain', all on different notes.

There you are in a marine world, in a good, salty and gallant little town, which once fought against the Saracens, against the Duke of Anjou, against the barbarian pirates, against the Constable of Bourbon, and Charles V, and the Duke of Savoy and the Duke of Épernon.

In 1637 the inhabitants, the forefathers of these peaceful bourgeois, drove away the Spanish fleet without any help, and

* De Suffren de Saint-Tropez (1729–88), famous French naval captain; he also served among the Knights Hospitallers of Malta and was made Bailli of the Order.

each year a reconstruction of that attack and that defence is carried out with astonishing vigour, filling the town with scuffles and clamour, and oddly recalling the great popular entertainments of the Middle Ages. In 1813 the town repulsed in the same way an English flotilla sent against them.

Today they fish. They fish for tuna, sardines, bass, rock lobsters, all the pretty fish from this blue sea, and by themselves they supply one part of the coast.

As I stepped ashore after I had washed and dressed, I heard midday strike, and I noticed two old clerks, notary's or lawyer's clerks, on their way to lunch, like two old beasts of burden unharnessed for a moment to eat their oats from the bottom of a sack.

Oh freedom! Freedom – the only hope, the only dream, the only happiness! Of all poor creatures, from every group of individuals, every category of worker, of all the men who every day carry on the hard battle to survive, those are the most to be pitied and the most deprived of support.

It is not believed. No one is aware of it. They are powerless to complain, they cannot rebel, they remain bound and gagged in their misery, the humiliating misery of pen-pushers. They are educated, they have studied law, perhaps they have a degree.

How I love Jules Vallès's dedication: 'To all those who, nourished on Greek and Latin, died of starvation.'

Do people know what they earn, these paupers? From eight hundred to fifteen hundred francs a year!*

Clerks in dark law offices, clerks in the great Ministries, you must read every morning over the door of the gloomy prison Dante's famous phrase: 'Abandon hope, all ye who enter here.'

They make their way in for the first time at the age of twenty, to remain there until they are sixty or more, and during this long time nothing happens. The whole of their existence flows by in the little dark office, always the same, lined with green boxes. They go in young, at a time of vigorous hope. They

---

* Maupassant had personal experience; elsewhere (*Chroniques I*, p. 376) he included comparisons: a good mason earned 2500 francs a year, a workman with any kind of special skill could earn 3700 francs a year.

come out old, near to death. All the harvest of memories throughout a life, unexpected events, tender or tragic love affairs, adventurous journeys, all the chance happenings of a free existence, these are unknown to these galley slaves. All the days, the weeks, the months, the seasons, the years are alike. They arrive at the same time, they have lunch at the same time, they leave at the same time, and they do that from the age of twenty to sixty. There are only four milestones: marriage, the birth of the first child, the death of their father and their mother. Nothing else – oh, yes, excuse me – promotions. They know nothing about ordinary life, nothing about the world! They are even ignorant of joyful sunny days in the streets, and wanderings in the countryside, because they are never let out before the appointed hour. They are incarcerated at eight o'clock in the morning; the prison opens at six o'clock, just as night falls. Though as compensation, for a fortnight a year, they do have the right – a right, moreover, which is argued about, bargained for, grudged – to stay shut up at home. For where could they go without money?

The roofer climbs up to the sky, the coachman roams the streets, the engine-driver travels through woods, plains, mountains, going continually from the town walls to the wide blue horizon of the sea. The clerk never leaves his office, this living creature's coffin, and in the same little mirror where he saw himself young with his fair moustache the day he arrived, he looks at himself bald with his white beard on the day he is turned out. So it is all over, life has closed down, the future barred. How could you be there already? How can you have got old like that without anything at all happening, without any surprise in life ever having shaken you? All the same, it is so. Make way for the young, for the young clerks!

So they leave, more wretched still, and they die almost at once from the sudden break in the long, relentless habit of going daily to the office, with the same movements, the same actions, the same tasks at the same times.

The moment I went into the hotel to have lunch I was given an appalling pile of letters and newspapers that awaited me, and my heart sank as though some disaster threatened. I have a fear and a hatred of letters; they are ties. These little squares of paper that bear my name seem to make, as I tear them open, a sound like chains, the sound of chains attaching me to the living people I have known, and continue to know.

Even though written by different hands, all of them say, 'Where are you? What are you doing? Why disappear like that without saying where you are going? Who are you hiding with?' Another adds, 'How can you expect people to be attached to you if you are always running away from your friends; it's even hurtful for them. . . .'

Well, they had better not get attached to me! For people cannot understand affection without adding to it a note of possession and dictatorship. It seems that relationships are not able to exist without bringing obligations, sensitivities and a certain amount of servitude along with them. Once you have smiled at the polite overtures of a stranger, this stranger has a hold over you, is concerned about what you are doing and reproaches you for neglect. If we get as far as friendship, each one imagines himself to have rights; relationships become duties, and the ties that unite us seem to end in slip-knots.

This feeling of insecurity, this suspicious, checking, clutching jealousy in people who have met and think they are chained to each other because they found each other attractive, is only due to the driving fear of solitude which haunts men on this earth.

Each one of us, feeling the void around him, the unfathomable void where his heart is moved, where his thoughts flounder, goes off like a madman, arms open wide, lips ready, looking for someone to clasp. He embraces to the right and to the left, randomly, with no knowledge, observation or understanding, so as to be no longer alone. He seems to say, as soon as he has shaken their hand, 'Now you belong to me a little. You owe me something of yourself, your life, your thoughts, your time.' That is why so many people believe they love each other when they are completely ignorant about each other; so many people go hand in hand or mouth on mouth without even having taken the time to look at each other. They have to love each other, so as not to be alone any more; it may be friendly love, affectionate love, but they must love for ever. They say it, swear it, they are carried away, they throw their whole heart into an unknown heart met the day before, their whole soul into a passing soul whose face appealed to them. It is from this haste to be united that so many misunderstandings, surprises, mistakes and dramas are born.

Just as we remain alone, in spite of all our trying, in the same way we stay free in spite of all the embraces.

No one, ever, belongs to anyone else. You participate, unable to help yourself, in the flirtatious or passionate game of possession, but you never give yourself. Man, provoked by the need to master someone, has set up tyranny, slavery and marriage. He can kill, torture, imprison, but human will always escapes from him, even when it has momentarily agreed to submit.

Do mothers possess their children? Doesn't the little creature, hardly out of the womb, start to cry to say what he wants, to tell of his solitude and to state his independence?

Does a woman ever belong to you? Do you know what she is thinking, even if she adores you? Kiss her body, go into a trance on her lips. One word from your mouth or from hers, a single word, is enough to put implacable hatred between you.

All feelings of affection lose their charm if they become authoritarian. From the fact that I enjoy seeing and talking to someone, does it follow that I should be allowed to know what he is doing and what he likes?

The seething activity in towns great and small, in all social groups, the unpleasant, envious, backbiting and slanderous curiosity, the constant interest in the acquaintances and affections of others, the gossip and the scandal, do they not all come from our pretension to supervise other people's conduct, as though they all belonged to us in different degrees? In fact we imagine we have rights over them, over their life, for we want to organize it like our own, rights over their thoughts, for we require them to be of the same nature as our own, over their opinions, for we cannot tolerate them being different from ours, rights over their reputation, for we require it to be in accordance with our principles, and over their behaviour, for we become indignant when it does not obey our morality.

I was having lunch at the end of a long table in the Bailli de Suffren Hotel, reading my letters and my newspapers, when I was disturbed by the noisy remarks of half a dozen men sitting at the far end.

They were commercial travellers. They were talking about everything with conviction, with authority, with levity, with scorn, and they gave me a clear feeling of what the French mind is, that is to say the average understanding, reasoning, logic and wit in France. One of them, tall with a mop of red hair, was wearing the military medal and a lifesaving medal – a brave man. A little fat one was making puns incessantly, and laughing heartily himself before he had given the others time to understand them. A man with close-cropped hair was reorganizing the army and the judiciary, reforming the laws and the Constitution, defining the ideal Republic for his wine salesman's mind. Two neighbours were greatly enjoying themselves as they were telling each other of their amorous exploits, behind-the-counter adventures, or servant girls they had won.

I could see in them all of France, the legendary, witty, changeable, bold and chivalrous France. These men were typical of their race, everyday types that I would only need to romanticize a little to rediscover the Frenchman as he appears in the eyes of history, that ardent and lying old lady.

Ours is really a very amusing race, due to very particular qualities which are found nowhere else.

It is our changeableness first of all which so spiritedly diversifies our customs and our institutions. It makes the past history of our country appear to be an amazing adventure story whose 'to be followed in our next' is always full of the unexpected, of drama and comedy, of the terrible or the ludicrous. You may well be angry or indignant, according to your opinions, but it is quite certain that no history in the world is more amusing or more eventful than ours.

From the point of view of pure art – and why not allow

this particular and dispassionate point of view in politics as in literature? – it is unrivalled. What could be more curious and more astonishing than the events that have come about only in this last century?*

What will we see tomorrow? This waiting for the unexpected, is it not fundamentally delightful? Everything is possible with us, even the most unlikely absurdities and the most tragic adventures. Can anything surprise us? When a country has had the likes of Joan of Arc and Napoleon, it can be supposed to have miraculous soil.

Then again, we love women; we love them a great deal, with passion and with delicacy, with wit and with respect. Our chivalry cannot be compared to anything in any other country.

The man who keeps in his heart the chivalrous flame of the past few centuries surrounds women with an affection which is deep, gentle, emotional and aware all at the same time. He likes everything about them, everything which comes from them, everything they are, everything they do. He likes their clothes, their ornaments, their finery, their tricks, their naïvety, their deceptions, their lies and their kindnesses. He likes them all, the rich as well as the poor, the young and even the old, brunettes, blondes, fat, thin. He is at ease near them, among them. He could stay there indefinitely, without tiring, without boredom, happy simply in their presence.

He knows, from the first words, by a look, by a smile, how to show them that he likes them, how to catch their attention, sharpen their desire to please, make them use all their seduction on him. A lively sympathy, an instinctive friendship are at once established between them and him, as if their characters and natures were related.

A sort of chivalrous and flirtatious battle begins between them and him, a mysterious and warlike knot of friendship is tied, an obscure kinship of heart and mind is secured.

---

* Maupassant first wrote these words in 1884 (*Chroniques II*, p. 389), so the previous 100 years included three republics, four monarchies, two empires and more than the one Revolution, to put it at its very simplest.

He knows how to say what pleases them, make them understand what he is thinking, he shows them without ever shocking them, without ever offending their frail and changeable modesty, that he feels a discreet and sharp desire, always awake in his eyes, always trembling on his lips, always on fire in his veins. He is their friend and their slave, the servitor of their fancies and the admirer of their person. He is ready at their call, to help them, to defend them as secret allies do. He would like to devote himself to them, to those he hardly knows, those he does not know, those he has never seen.

He asks of them nothing but a little kind affection, a little trust or a little interest, a touch of gracefulness or even mischievous treachery.

In the street he likes the woman who passes by, whose glance caresses him. He likes the young girl, hatless, a blue ribbon in her hair, a flower at her breast, crossing the crowded pavements with slow or hurried step, her eyes timid or bold. He likes the strangers he comes across, the little shopkeeper daydreaming on her doorstep, the nonchalant beauty lying back in her open carriage.

As soon as he is faced with a woman, his heart is moved and his mind awakes. He thinks of her, speaks for her, tries to please her and to make her see that she pleases him. Expressions of affection come to his lips, caresses in his looks, he wants to kiss her hand, to touch her dress. To him, women embellish the world and give life its charm. He likes to sit at their feet simply for the pleasure of being there, he likes to catch their eye, just to seek veiled and fleeting thoughts, he likes to hear their voice solely because it is a woman's voice.

It is through them and for them that the French man has learned to converse, and always to be witty.

What is conversation? What an enigma! It is the art of never seeming tedious, of knowing how to say everything in an interesting way, of pleasing with anything to hand, of charming with nothing at all.

How can you define this vivid skimming over things with words, this batting to and fro of flexible words, this kind of slight smile of ideas which conversation should be?

The French alone in the world have wit, and they are alone in appreciating and understanding it. They have a wit that passes by and a wit that stays, a street wit and a bookish wit.

What remains is wit in the wide sense, this great breath of irony or gaiety spread over our population from the moment it thinks and speaks; it is the awe-inspiring verve of Montaigne and of Rabelais, the irony of Voltaire, of Beaumarchais, of Saint-Simon and the miraculous laugh of Molière. The quip, the witticism is the very small change of that wit. Yet it is still one side of it, a very individual characteristic of our national intelligence. It is one of its more lively charms. It makes up the sceptical gaiety of our Parisian life, the likeable insouciance of our ways. It is part of our charm.

These joking games were once in verse; today they are in prose. According to the age they are called epigrams, conceits, *bons mots*, gibes, suggestive jokes. They run through the town and the salons, come up everywhere, on the boulevard as they do in Montmartre, and those of Montmartre are often as good as those of the boulevard. They appear in the newspapers; from one end of France to the other they make people laugh, for we do know how to laugh.

Why does one word any more than another, the unexpected, bizarre juxtaposition of two terms, two ideas or even two sounds, any old absurdity, an unexpected *non sequitur*, why do they open the floodgates of gaiety, suddenly, like an exploding mine, and make all Paris and the whole country burst into laughter?

Why will all the French start laughing, when all the English and all the Germans will not understand what is amusing us? Why? It is simply because we are French, that we have a French perception, that we have the delightful gift of laughter.

Besides, for us it is enough to have a little wit to govern. Good humour takes the place of genius, a jest sanctifies a man and makes him historically great. All the rest is of little importance. People love those who amuse them and forgive those who make them laugh.

Only one glance at the past of our country will make us see that the renown of our great men has only ever come about through a happy choice of words. The most detestable princes have become popular with pleasant jokes, repeated and remembered from century to century.

The French throne is supported by heraldic devices of scrolls of doggerel.

Words, words, nothing but words, ironic or heroic, funny or ribald, words come to the surface of our history and give the impression of an anthology of puns.

Clovis, the Christian king, cried out as he heard the Passion read, 'Why wasn't I there with my Franks!'

This prince, in order to reign alone, butchered his allies and his relatives and committed every crime imaginable. Nevertheless he is considered to be a pious and civilizing monarch.

'Why wasn't I there with my Franks!'

We would have known nothing about good King Dagobert if the song had not told us, no doubt in error, of some oddities in his life.

Pépin, wanting to turn King Childéric off the throne, asked Pope Zacharie this insidious question, 'Which of us is more worthy to reign, the one who worthily carries out all the functions of a king, without having the title, or the one who has the title without knowing how to govern?'

What do we know of Louis VI? Nothing. I beg your pardon: at the battle of Brenneville, as an Englishman put his hand on him shouting, 'The King is taken!', this prince, thoroughly French, replied, 'Do you not know that you can never take a King, even in chess!'

Louis IX, although he was a saint, leaves us not a single word to remember. So his reign seems to us horribly boring, full of prayers and penitence.

Philippe VI, that simpleton, beaten and wounded at Crécy, went and knocked on the door of the château of Arbroie crying, 'Open up, it is the fortune of France!' We are still grateful for these melodramatic words.

Jean II, a prisoner of the Prince of Wales, said to him, with knightly good grace and the chivalry of a French troubadour, 'I counted on giving you supper today, but fate determines otherwise and wishes me to sup with you.' One cannot be more gracious in adversity.

'It is not up to the King of France to avenge the quarrels of the Duke of Orléans,' declared Louis XII generously. There, truly, you have a great royal saying, one worthy of being retained by all princes.

François I, that great booby, petticoat chaser and unlucky general, saved his reputation by surrounding his name with an imperishable halo by writing these few superb words to his mother, after defeat at Pavia, 'All is lost, madame, save honour.'

Don't these words seem as good as a victory today? Don't they illustrate the prince better than the conquest of a kingdom? We have forgotten the names of most of the great battles carried on in that far-off age; will anyone ever forget 'All is lost, save honour . . .'?

Henri IV! Hail, gentlemen, here is the master! Crafty, a sceptic, sharp, with a false bonhomie, with a cunning like no one else, more misleading than you could suppose, debauched, a drunkard and believing in nothing, he knew, with a few well-chosen words, how to create the admirable reputation in the eyes of history of a chivalrous, generous king, and a decent, loyal and upright man.

Oh! the fraud, how well that one knew how to play on human stupidity.

'Hang yourself, good Crillon, we have won without you!' After words like that a general is always ready to hang himself or to kill for his master.

At the moment of joining the famous battle of Ivry: 'My children, if you lack standards, rally to my white-plumed helmet; you will always find it in the path of honour and victory!' Was it possible he was not always victorious, he who knew how to speak like that to his captains and his troops?

He wanted Paris, this sceptic king; he wanted it but he had to choose between his faith and the beautiful town. 'Bah!' he murmured, 'Paris is well worth a mass!' So he changed his religion as he would change his clothes. All the same, isn't it true that the words made the thing acceptable? 'Paris is well worth a mass!' made those with wit laugh, and people were not too angry.

Did he not become the patron of fathers of families by asking the Spanish ambassador, who found him playing at horses with the Dauphin, 'Ambassador, are you a father?'

The Spaniard replied, 'Yes, sire.'

'In that case,' said the King, 'I will carry on.'

But he conquered for eternity the French heart, the bourgeois heart and the popular heart, with the most beautiful saying ever uttered by a prince, a genius of a saying, full of depth, bonhomie, trickery and good sense.

'If God spares me, I would like there to be no peasant in my kingdom so poor that he cannot put a chicken in the pot on Sundays.'

It is with words like that that enthusiastic and simple-minded crowds are taken over, governed, dominated. With a few words, Henri IV has drawn his countenance for posterity. You cannot say his name without immediately having a vision of white plumes and smelling the chicken in the pot.

Louis XIII had no sayings. This sad king had a sad reign.

Louis XIV gave us the formula for absolute personal power: 'L'État, c'est moi!' He showed the extent of royal arrogance in its most complete flowering: 'I almost had to wait.' He gave an example of the high-sounding political sayings which make alliances between two peoples, 'There are no more Pyrenees.'

His whole reign is there in those few words.

Louis XV, the corrupt, elegant and witty king, has left behind a charming touch of his sovereign insouciance, 'Après moi, le déluge!'

If Louis XVI had had the wit to leave a saying he might have saved the monarchy. With a quip, might he not have avoided the guillotine?

Napoleon I threw fistfuls of all the necessary words into the hearts of his soldiers.

Napoleon III suppressed all the future anger of the nation with a short phrase as he promised, 'The Empire means peace!' The Empire means peace! Superb statement, wonderful lie! After having said that he could declare war on the whole of Europe with nothing to fear from his people. He had found a formula that was simple, neat, striking, capable of sticking in the mind, and against which the facts could no longer prevail.

He made war on China, Mexico, Russia, Austria, on everyone. What did it matter? Some people still speak convincingly of the eighteen years of tranquillity he gave us. 'The Empire means peace.'

It was also with words, words more mortal than shot, that Henri Rochefort felled the Empire, puncturing it with his shafts, tearing and shredding it.

Marshal MacMahon himself has left us a souvenir of his passage through power, 'Here I am, here I stay!', and it was through a saying of Gambetta's that he in his turn was kicked out, 'Give in or get out.'

With these two verbs, more powerful than a revolution, more formidable than barricades, more invincible than an army, more to be feared than all the votes, the people's tribune overcame the soldier, crushed his glory, annihilated his power and his prestige.

As for those governing us today, they will fall, for they have no wit; they will fall, because on a day of danger, the day of an uprising, the day of the inevitable turning point, they will not know how to make France laugh and disarm her.

Of all these historical sayings, there are not ten that are authentic. What does it matter, as long as they are believed to have been said by those supposed to have said them, for in the words of the popular song: *In the land of the hunchback/ You must be one/ Or appear to be one.*

Meanwhile the commercial travellers were now talking about the emancipation of women, of their rights and of the new position they wanted to have in society.

Some approved, others were angry; the little fat one made jokes without respite, and at the same time terminated both the meal and the discussion with this quite amusing anecdote:

'Recently', he said, 'a great meeting took place in England, where this question had been discussed. A speaker had just marshalled numerous arguments in favour of women, when he finished with this phrase, "To sum up, gentlemen, the difference that distinguishes man from woman is really quite a little one."

'A loud, convinced, enthusiastic voice rose from the crowd and cried, "Hurrah for the little difference!"'

Since the weather was very good this morning, I left for the Carthusian monastery of La Verne.

Two memories led me to this ruin – the feeling of infinite solitude and unforgettable sadness I had felt in the abandoned cloister, and then that of an old couple of country folk, whose house I had been taken to the year before by a friend who was showing me around the region of the Maures.

Sitting in a cart, as the road would soon become impassable for a vehicle with springs, first of all I followed the bay to its far end. I could see on the opposite bank the pine woods where the development company is going to try another resort; the spot moreover is admirable, and the entire area is magnificent. After that the road plunges into the mountains and soon passes through the village of Cogolin. A little farther on I left it to take a bumpy way which was like a long rut. A river, or rather a big stream, flowed beside it and every hundred yards it cut across this hollow, flooded it, went off a little, came back mistaken again, abandoned its bed and drowned the road, then it fell into a ditch, wandered off in a stony field, appeared suddenly to be well behaved and followed its course for a while, but, all at once taken by an abrupt caprice, it rushed once more into the path, which it transformed into a pond, and into which the horse plunged up to its breast and the high cart up to the chassis.

No more houses, here and there a charcoal-burner's hut. The very poorest live in holes. Can you imagine that men live in holes, that they live there all the year round, breaking up wood and burning it to get charcoal from it, eating bread and onions, drinking water and sleeping like rabbits in their burrows, at the bottom of a small hollow scooped out of the granite? What is more, someone has just discovered, in the midst of these unexplored valleys, a hermit, a real hermit, hidden there for thirty years, unsuspected by everyone, even by the forest keepers.

The existence of this wild man, revealed by I know not who, was no doubt mentioned to the driver of the diligence, who spoke about it to the postmaster, who chatted to the manager or manageress of the telegraph, who expressed amazement to the editor of some *Petit Midi* or other, who wrote a sensational article reprinted by all the papers in Provence.

The police went into action and discovered the hermit – what is more, without interfering with his peace, which proves that he must have kept his identity papers. Then, excited by this news, a photographer set out in his turn, wandered three days and three nights across the mountains, and ended by taking a photograph of someone, the real hermit say some, a false one declare others.

However, last year the friend who showed me this extraordinary area showed me two creatures who were surely more peculiar than the poor devil who came to hide remorse, grief, incurable despair, or perhaps simple boredom with life, in this impenetrable forest.

This is how he found them. Wandering on horseback across these valleys, he came across some kind of prosperous holding, with vines, fields and a farmhouse, humble but habitable.

He went in. A woman greeted him, aged about seventy, a countrywoman. The man, seated under a tree, got up and came over in welcome. 'He is deaf,' she said.

He was a big old man of about eighty, amazingly strong, upright and handsome.

They employed a man and a servant girl. My friend, a little surprised to find these unusual people in this deserted area, enquired about them. They had been there a long time; they were much respected and they were thought to be well off, well off for simple folk.

He came back to see them several times and little by little he became friendly with the woman. He brought her newspapers, books, and was surprised to find that she had ideas, or rather the remnants of ideas, which did not seem to fit with her station. However she was not literary, nor intelligent, nor witty, but seemed to have, in the depths of her memory, traces of forgotten thoughts, the slumbering recollection of a former education.

One day she asked him his name.

'I am called Count X . . .,' he said.

She responded, moved by one of these obscure vanities lying deep down in all minds, 'I, too, am noble!'

Then she went on, speaking undoubtedly for the first time of this matter which was so old, unknown to everyone.

'I am the daughter of a colonel. My husband was a non-commissioned officer in Papa's regiment. I fell in love with him, and we ran off together.'

'And you came here?'

'Yes, we went into hiding.'

'And you have never seen your family again?'

'Oh, no! Remember, my husband was a deserter.'

'You have never written to anyone?'

'Oh, no!'

'And you have heard nothing about anyone in your family, not your father or your mother?'

'Oh, no! Maman was dead.'

This woman had retained something childlike, the naïve air of those who fling themselves at love as they would over a precipice.

He asked again, 'You have never told that to anyone?'

'Oh, no! I am saying it now because Maurice is deaf. While he could hear I wouldn't have dared speak about it. And then I have only ever seen the local people since I ran away.'

'Have you at least been happy?'

'Oh, yes! Very happy. He has made me very happy. I have never had any regrets.'

Last year I in my turn had gone to see this woman, this couple, as you would go to see a miraculous relic. Sad, surprised, admiring and repelled, I had contemplated this girl who had followed this man, this bumpkin, attracted by his uniform of a galloping hussar, and who later, beneath his humble rags, had gone on seeing him with the blue hussar's tunic on his back, the sabre at his side and wearing the spurred boots that jingle.

Meanwhile she had become countrified herself. She had become used to this life at the back of beyond with no charms, no luxury, no delicacy of any kind; she had bent to these simple ways – and she still loved him. She had become a woman of the people, with a bonnet and a rough skirt. She ate a broth of cabbage, potato and fat bacon from an earthen plate on a wooden table, sitting on a straw chair. She slept on a straw mattress at his side.

She had never thought of anything but him! She had no regrets for the finery, nor the silks, nor the elegance, nor for the softness of the chairs, nor the scented warmth of the rooms with their hangings, nor the downy quilts into which the body plunges to rest. She had never needed anything but him! As long as he was there she wanted nothing. She had abandoned life, still young, both the world and those who had brought her up, who loved her. She had come, alone with him, to this wild valley. He had been everything to her, everything one desires, everything one dreams about, everything constantly waited for, everything endlessly hoped for. He had filled her existence with happiness from one end to the other. She could not have been happier.

Now, for the second time, I was going to see her again with the astonishment and the vague contempt that I could feel for her within me.

She lived on the other side of the mountain to the Carthusian monastery, near the Hyères road, where another vehicle would be waiting for me, since the rut we had been following suddenly stopped and became a simple track, only accessible on foot or to mules.

So I began to go up, alone, on foot and at a slow pace. I was in a delightful forest, a real Corsican *maquis*, a fairytale wood with flowering creepers, aromatic plants with powerful scents, and magnificent great trees. The bits of granite in the path gleamed and rolled, and through the gaps in the branches I suddenly noticed large dark valleys extending farther than I could see, all green.

I was hot, the blood was flowing keenly through my body, I could feel it running in my veins, almost burning, fast, lively, rhythmical, stirring as a song, the great merry and simple song of life which quickens in the sun. I was happy, I was strong, I quickened my step, climbing the rocks, jumping, running, from moment to moment discovering a wider area, a huge network of deserted valleys from which the smoke of not one single roof was rising.

Then I reached the summit, overlooked by other summits still higher, and after a few detours I saw on the side of the mountain opposite, behind an immense chestnut wood which went from the top to the bottom of a valley, a black ruin, a heap of dark stones and ancient buildings supported by high arches. In order to reach it you had to go round a wide ravine and through the chestnut wood. The trees, old as the abbey, were living on after its death, huge, maimed, dying. Some had fallen, no longer able to support that age, others, decapitated, were no more than a hollow trunk in which ten men could hide; they had the air of a mighty army of antique giants struck by lightning and still climbing up to assault the sky. They had a smell of the centuries and of moulds, the ancient life of rotted roots in this fantastic wood where nothing flowered any more at the foot of these giants. Between the grey trunks was hard, stony soil, with the occasional patch of grass.

There were two springs, enclosed to make drinking fountains for cattle.

I came up to the abbey and discovered all the old buildings; the oldest date from the twelfth century, and the most recent were lived in by a family of herdsmen.

In the first courtyard you could see from the traces of animals that a vestige of life still haunted the place, then after having crossed crumbling rooms like those in all ruins, you arrived in the cloister, a long and low walk still covered by a roof, surrounding a meadow of brambles and tall grasses. Nowhere in the world have I felt the weight of melancholy so heavy as in this ancient and sinister monks' ambulatory. Certainly the shape of the arches and the proportions of the place contributed to this feeling, to this tightening of the heart, and they saddened the mind through the eye, just as the harmonious line of a cheerful monument rejoices the sight. The man who built this retreat must have been in despair to have been able to create this desolate walk. You wanted to cry between these walls, to cry and to moan; you wanted to suffer, to uncover the wounds in your heart, and to increase, to enlarge to an infinite degree all the griefs compressed within.

I climbed through a gap to look at the countryside outside and I understood – there was nothing around us, nothing but death. Behind the abbey there was a mountain going up to the sky, around the ruins was the chestnut wood, and in front a valley, and farther off other valleys – pines, pines, an ocean of pines and, right to the horizon, still more pines on the mountain tops. I went away.

After that I went through a wood of cork oaks, where the other year I had had a moving and powerful surprise.

It had been a grey day, in October, at the time when they come to tear the bark off these trees to make corks. They are skinned like that from the foot up to the first branches, and the bare trunk becomes red, a blood red like a skinned limb. They have bizarre, twisted shapes, the look of crippled people, of contorted epileptics, and I had suddenly felt as though I was cast into a forest of the tortured, in a bloody forest in hell where men have roots, where bodies deformed by torture looked like trees, where life constantly poured out, in endless suffering, through these bleeding wounds, and which made me wince and feel faint as nervous people do at the sudden sight of blood, an unexpected glimpse of a man who is crushed, or fallen from a roof. This sensation was so vivid, and this emotion was so strong that I believed I heard wails, far away, heart-rending, innumerable cries and, having touched one of these trees to steady my heart, I believed I saw, I did see as I turned it towards me, that my hand was all red.

Today they are cured – until the next stripping.

Then at last I saw the road that passes near the farm that sheltered the long, happy life of the non-commissioned officer of hussars and the colonel's daughter.

From far off I recognized the man, who was walking among his vines. So much the better; the woman would be alone in the house.

The servant was washing the front door step.

'Is your mistress here?' I said.

She replied with a strange air, with the accent of the Midi, 'No, sir, it's six months now that she's gone.'

'She is dead?'

'Yes, sir.'

'What of?'

The woman hesitated, then murmured, 'She's dead, well, she's dead.'

'But what of?'

'Well, from a fall!'

'From a fall? Where was that?'

'From the window.'

I gave her twenty sous. 'Tell me about it,' I said.

No doubt she very much wanted to talk, no doubt also she must often have repeated this story in six months, for she told it at length like something well known and unchanging. I learned that for thirty years the man, the old, deaf man, had had a mistress in the neighbouring village, and that his wife, having learned of it by chance from a carter who was passing and who chatted about it without knowing who she was, had run off desperate and shrieking up to the granary, then jumped out of the window, probably without thinking of what she was doing, but driven mad by the horrible grief of the shock

which threw her onwards with an irresistible thrust, like a whip that cracks and lacerates. She had climbed the stair, gone through the door and without knowing, without being able to stop her flight, continuing to run forwards, she had jumped into the void.

As for him – he had known nothing, he still did not know, and he would never know because he was deaf. His wife was dead, that was all. Everyone had to die sometime. I could see him in the distance giving orders to the workers with signs.

Then I saw the cart waiting for me in the shade of a tree, and I went back to Saint-Tropez.

I was going to bed last night, even though it was scarcely nine o'clock, when I was given a telegram.

A friend, one of those I am fond of, said, 'I am in Monte Carlo for four days, and I have been sending you messages to all the ports on the coast. So come and join me.'

There I was with the wish to see him, the wish to talk, to laugh, to discuss the world, things, people, to slander, to gossip, to judge, to blame, to imagine, to chat, flaming up in me like fire. That very morning I would have been exasperated by this summons and this evening I was delighted by it; I would have liked to be there already, to see the big restaurant full of people, to hear the murmur of voices where the numbers of roulette dominate all the phrases like the *Dominus vobiscum* does in church services.

I called Bernard. 'We will leave for Monaco at four o'clock in the morning,' I said.

He replied philosophically, 'If the weather is good, sir.'

'It will be good.'

'It's just that the barometer is falling.'

'Nonsense! It'll go up again.'

The sailor smiled his sceptical smile. I went to bed and I went to sleep.

It was I who woke the men. It was dark; a few clouds hid the sky. The barometer had gone down more.

The two sailors shook their heads with a distrustful air.

I repeated, 'Nonsense! it will be fine. Come on, let's go!'

Bernard said, 'When I am able to see out to sea, I know what I am doing; but here, in this port, at the far end of this bay, you know nothing, sir, you can see nothing; there could be a raging sea and we wouldn't know.'

I replied, 'The barometer has gone down, so we won't have an east wind. Now if we have a west wind we would be able to shelter at Agay, which is six or seven miles.'

The men did not seem reassured; all the same, they got ready to leave.

'Shall we put the dinghy on deck?' asked Bernard.

'No. You'll see, it will be fine. Keep it on tow, behind us.'

A quarter of an hour later we were leaving the port and we were entering the passage out of the bay, pushed by a light and intermittent breeze.

I laughed. 'Well! You see it is fine.'

We had soon passed the black and white tower built on the sunken reef of the Rabiou and, even though protected by Cap Camarat which advances in the distance into the open sea, and whose flashing light appeared from moment to moment, the *Bel-Ami* was already being lifted by long, slow, powerful waves, these hills of water which advance one behind the other, silently, smoothly, with no spray, menacing without being angry, frightening in their tranquillity.

You could see nothing, you could only feel the rising and falling of the yacht on this moving and shadowy sea. Bernard said, 'There has been a strong wind at sea during the night, sir. We will be lucky if we arrive without trouble.'

A clear day was breaking on the moving horde of waves, and we all three looked out to sea, to see if the squall might start again. Meanwhile the boat was going swiftly, with the wind aft, pushed by the sea. Already we had Agay abeam, and we considered whether we should head for Cannes in anticipation of bad weather, or for Nice, passing seaward of the islands. Bernard preferred to go in to Cannes, but as the breeze was no stronger, I decided in favour of Nice.

For three hours everything went well, even though the poor little yacht rolled like a cork in the heavy seas.

Anyone who has not seen this ocean swell, this mountainous sea which goes on its swift and heavy way, separated by valleys that are moving on second by second, filled in and re-formed incessantly, cannot guess at, cannot suspect the mysterious, formidable, terrifying and magnificent power of the waves.

Our little dinghy was following far behind us at the end of a forty-metre line, in this dancing, liquid chaos. We constantly lost sight of it, then suddenly it would reappear at the crest of a wave, swimming like a big, white bird.

Just opposite, Cannes was sunk in its bay, and Saint-Honorat with its tower standing up in the waves, and in front of us the Cap d'Antibes.

The breeze freshened little by little, and on the crest of the waves white horses appeared, those snowy white horses that go so fast, incessantly hunting, with no huntsman and no hounds, under the infinite sky.

Bernard said to me, 'It'll be a near thing if we reach Antibes.' Indeed the seas were coming, breaking over us, with a violent, indescribable noise. The sudden squalls buffeted us, threw us into the yawning holes from which we emerged, as we righted ourselves, terribly shaken.

The peak of the sail had been raised, but the boom touched the waves at every roll of the boat, seeming ready to tear out the mast which would fly off with its sail, leaving us alone, floating, lost in the raging water.

Bernard shouted to me, 'The dinghy, sir.'

I turned round. A monstrous wave had filled it, rolled it, enveloped it in its foam as though it were devouring it and, breaking the painter that attached it to us, kept it, half sunk, drowned, a conquered, vanquished prey, which it was going to throw on the rocks on the far-off cape.

The minutes seemed like hours. Nothing could be done, we had to go on, we had to reach the headland in front of us and, once round it, we would be in its lee, saved.

At last, we reached it! Now the sea was calm, at one, protected by the long band of rocks and land that forms the Cap d'Antibes.

There was the port from which we had set out hardly more than a few days ago, though I could have believed we had been travelling for months, and we entered it as midday struck. The sailors, back home, were radiant, even though Bernard repeated every moment, 'Ah! sir, our poor little dinghy, it breaks my heart to have seen it perish like that.'

Then I took the four o'clock train to go and have dinner with my friend in the Principality of Monaco.

I would like to have the leisure to talk at length about this amazing state, which is not as big as a French village, but where you find an absolute ruler, some bishops, an army of Jesuits and seminarists bigger than that of the Prince, an artillery whose canons are almost written off, an etiquette more ceremonious than that of the late Louis XIV, notions of authority more despotic than William of Prussia, allied with a magnificent tolerance of the vices of humanity, which support the sovereign, the bishops, the Jesuits, the seminarists, the ministers, the army, the magistrature – everyone.

Moreover, let us salute this good and pacifist ruler who, with no fear of invasion or revolution, reigns peacefully over his happy little people in the midst of the ceremonial of a court where the traditions of the four bows, the twenty-six kisses of the hand and all the formulas once in use around the Great Dictators have been preserved intact.

Yet this monarch is neither bloodthirsty nor vindictive, and when he banishes, for he does banish, the measure is applied with infinite precautions.

Is proof required?

A determined gambler, on a day when he was out of luck, insulted the sovereign. He was expelled by decree. For a month he wandered around the edge of the forbidden paradise, fearing the sword of the archangel in the form of the gendarme's sabre. Finally one day he felt brave, crossed the frontier, was in the heart of the country in thirty seconds, and entered the Casino, but suddenly an official stopped him, 'Are you not banished, sir?'

'Yes, but I am leaving by the first train.'

'Oh! In that case, very well, sir, you may go in.'

Every week he came back, and every time the same official asked him the same question, to which he replied in the same fashion.

Can justice be more mild?

Though in one year recently a very serious and quite new situation came about in the principality. There was a murder.

A man, a Monégasque, and not one of these wandering foreigners who are encountered in their legions on this coast, a husband, killed his wife in a moment of anger.

Oh, yes, he killed her unreasonably, with no acceptable excuse. Strong feeling was unanimous in the principality.

The High Court gathered to judge this exceptional case (there had never before been a murder), and the wretch was unanimously condemned to death. The outraged sovereign ratified the decision.

It only remained to execute the criminal. Then a difficulty arose. The country possessed neither executioner nor guillotine.

What should be done? On the advice of the Minister for Foreign Affairs the Prince began negotiations with the French government to obtain the loan of a cutter-off of heads, together with his machine.

There was then a great deal of deliberation in the Ministry in Paris. At last they replied by sending an account for the cost of moving the wooden framework and its operator. It all amounted to sixteen thousand francs.

His Majesty of Monaco thought he would find the operation very expensive; the assassin was certainly not worth that amount – sixteen thousand francs for a fool's neck! Oh, no!

So the same request was addressed to the Italian government. A king, a brother, would no doubt be less demanding than a republic.

The Italian government sent an estimate which amounted to twelve thousand francs.

Twelve thousand francs! It would be necessary to raise a tax, something new, a tax of two francs per inhabitant. That would be enough to bring unthinkable trouble on the state.

They thought of getting a simple soldier to decapitate the scoundrel, but the general, when consulted, replied hesitantly that perhaps his men were not sufficiently used to sharp weapons to carry out a task that required extensive experience of sabre handling.

So the Prince once more assembled the High Court and put this embarrassing case before it. They deliberated for a long time, without coming to any practical solution. Finally the presiding judge proposed that the death penalty should be commuted to life imprisonment, and the measure was passed.

However, they had no prison. One had to be arranged, and a gaoler was appointed to take delivery of the prisoner.

For six months everything went well. The captive slept all day on a straw mattress in his cell, and the guard did the same thing on a chair by the door as he watched the travellers pass by.

However the Prince is economical, to say the least, and he makes sure he sees an account of the smallest expenses in his state (it is not a long list). So he was given the bill for the costs concerning the setting up of this new appointment, the upkeep of the prison, the prisoner and the guard. The wages of the latter weighed heavily on the sovereign's budget.

At first he made a face, then when he thought that it could go on for ever (the condemned man was young), he warned his Minister of Justice that he would have to take measures to remove this expense.

The Minister consulted the President of the Court, and both of them agreed that the cost of the gaoler should be removed. The prisoner, who would be requested to guard himself, could hardly fail to escape, which would resolve the question to everyone's satisfaction.

So the gaoler was returned to his family and a kitchen help from the palace was simply required to deliver, morning and evening, the guilty man's food, but the latter made no effort to regain his freedom.

One day, however, since they had neglected to provide him with food, he was seen to turn up tranquilly to ask for it. From then on, so as to spare the cook, he got into the habit of coming at mealtimes to eat in the palace with the staff, with whom he became friendly.

After his lunch he would go and take a walk as far as Monte Carlo. Sometimes he would go into the Casino and risk five francs on the green baize. When he won he would treat himself to a good dinner in a well-known hotel, then he would go back to his prison, whose door he would carefully close from inside.

Not a single time did he sleep anywhere else.

The situation was becoming difficult, not for the condemned man, but for the judges. The Court met once more, and it was decided that the criminal would be invited to leave the State of Monaco.

When he was told of this decree he simply replied, 'You must be joking. Well, and what is to become of me then? I no longer have the means of existence. I've no more family. What do you expect me to do? I was condemned to death; you didn't execute me; I said nothing. Then I'm condemned to life imprisonment and put in the care of a gaoler. You took my guard away; I still said nothing. Today you want to hunt me from the country. Oh, no! I am a prisoner, your prisoner, judged and condemned by you. I am faithfully submitting to my punishment. I'm staying here.'

The High Court was astounded. The Prince flew into a terrible rage and ordered that action be taken. They deliberated once more.

Then it was decided that the guilty man would be offered a pension of six hundred francs to go and live abroad. He accepted it.

He rented a little patch five minutes away from the state of his former sovereign and lived happily off his land, cultivating a few vegetables and despising potentates.

However the Court of Monaco, having learned a little late from this example, decided to come to an agreement with the French government. Now it delivers to us its condemned men, whom we handle discreetly, for a modest consideration.

The document fixing the pension of the rascal and obliging him to leave Monégasque territory can be seen in the legal archives of the principality.

Opposite the Prince's palace rises up the rival establishment, Roulette. Yet there is no hatred, no hostility between the two, for the latter supports the former, who in turn protects it. An admirable, a unique example of two neighbouring and power-ful families living in peace in a little state, just the example to wipe out the memory of the Montagues and the Capulets. Here the princely house and there the gaming house, the old and the new society fraternizing to the sound of gold.

The Prince's salons are as difficult of access for foreigners as those of the Casino are open to them. I went into the latter.

The sound of money, continuous as the waves, a light, for-midable, profound sound, filled the ears as you entered, then it filled the soul, moved the heart, disturbed the mind, mad-dened thought. It can be heard everywhere, this noise that sings, cries out, calls, tempts, and tears apart.

Around the tables was a dreadful crowd of gamblers, the scum of society and of continents, mingling with princes, or future kings, society women, bourgeois, money lenders, bro-ken-down tarts; it was a mixture unique on earth, of men of all races, all castes, all kinds, from every background, a mu-seum of Russian, Brazilian, Chilean, Italian, Spanish, German *rastaquouères*, old women with big bags, young trollops with tiny handbags on their wrists containing some keys, a hand-kerchief and their three last coins of a hundred sous which are destined for the green baize when they think they feel lucky.

I came up to the last table and I saw – pale, frowning, set lips, her whole face contorted and ill humoured – the young woman from Agay Bay, the beautiful one who was in love in the sunny woods and the gentle moonlight. He, too, is there, sitting in front of her, nervous, his hand on a few gold *louis*.

'Put it on the first square,' she said.

He asked, in agony, 'All of it?'

'Yes, all of it.'

He placed the *louis* in a little pile.

The croupier made the wheel turn. The ball was rolling, dancing, stopping. 'Rien ne va plus,' came the voice, and went on after a second, 'Twenty-eight.'

The young woman shivered, and in a hard and clipped tone, 'Let's go.'

He got up and, without looking at her, followed her, and you could feel that something terrible had come between them.

Someone said, 'Goodbye, love. They don't have the air of getting on well today.'

A hand fell on my shoulder. I turned round. It was my friend.

. . . .

It only remains for me to ask pardon for having talked about myself like this. I wrote this journal of day-dreams for myself alone, or rather I took advantage of my solitude afloat to halt the wandering ideas that cross our minds like birds.

I have been asked to publish these pages with no aim, no construction, no art, which follow one upon another with no reason and suddenly end, with no motive, because a gust of wind ended my voyage.

I gave in to this request. Perhaps I am wrong.

APPENDICES

WAR

When I hear the word pronounced, 'war', I feel as appalled as if it were a question of witchcraft, of inquisition, of something far-off, ended, barbaric, monstrous, against nature.

War! Fighting! Killing! The massacre of men! And we have today, in our time, with our civilization, with the breadth of knowledge and the degree of philosophy which we suppose the human mind to have attained, we have schools where they learn to kill, to kill from far away, perfectly, many people at the same time, to kill poor devils of innocent men, who have family responsibilities and no criminal records. And the most astounding thing is that the whole of society finds it natural. And perhaps anyone other than Victor Hugo would have been insulted, shouted down, stoned if they had raised the cry:

Today, force is called violence and its judgement is beginning; war is being accused. Civilization, with the human race as plaintiff, is preparing the trial and mounting the great criminal case against the conquerors and the captains. . . . The people will come to understand that amplifying atrocities cannot diminish them. That if to kill is a crime,

117

killing large numbers cannot be an attenuating factor; that if to steal is shameful, invasion cannot be glory. . . . Ah! let us proclaim these absolute truths, let us dishonour war.

* * *

A very skilled artist in this respect, Monsieur de Moltke, responded one day to peace delegates with these strange words: 'War is holy, divinely instituted; it is one of the sacred laws of the world; it keeps alive in men all the great and noble ideas, honour, detachment, virtue, courage, and prevents them, in a word, from falling into the most hideous materialism' (it is astonishing he did not say naturalism).

So, to join a pack of two hundred thousand men, march night and day without rest, think about nothing, study nothing, learn nothing, read nothing, rot in filth, sleep in muck, live like perpetually stupefied brutes, pillage towns, burn villages, ruin the population, then meet another great mass of human meat, hurl yourself at it, make pools of blood, heaps of corpses, have arms or legs taken off, your brain reduced to pulp, and rot in a corner of a field while your wife and your children starve; that is what is called not falling into the most hideous materialism (or naturalism).

If we even had the practicality of savages, if we were to use this butchered flesh as food, if war was a means of provisioning for poor nations, if we exported salted soldier like America exports cows and pigs in tins, it would only be half evil. Sometimes you would expose women to the risk of eating a haunch of their husband, that's all. It would still be the great battle for life, the right to kill to eat, which we exercise over animals. But no. We butcher for pleasure, for honour, and we waste all these dead bodies; their only use is to give us plague and cholera. For shame then! The real savage is the civilized man. He is a monster. The cannibal, on the contrary, is logical; I feel no scorn for him, because he acts according to his nature, unmodified by civilization.

Yet ask a gold-braided general what he thinks of the Kanaks who eat men!

All these arguments and this indignation are overdone, over-emphatic, as regards the little ornamental war we are treating ourselves to on the coast of Africa.*

However, regarding this war to entertain the ladies, I wonder, with a combination of anxiety and joy, if someone somewhere, beginning with the Minister for War (who has the air of being quite astonished by what is going on), suspects what is going to occur.

On the contrary, I am convinced that no one rightly knows what could happen if we go and attack Tunis or the Kroumirs, to conquer or simply to protect our frontiers.

Could the campaign have been planned by General Boum?

We had a nasty pimple, Tunis. It could have been cauterized once and for all, and finished with. Not at all; it is being scratched, it is being scratched so much and so well that it is becoming erysipelas. Then a few bandits kill a few men on our frontier, and here we are with the whole population in an uproar. A thrill runs from one end to the other of this gullible country. They murmur, 'War! War! Tunis, Roustan, Maccio, Roustan!'[†]

Then all the bourgeois, carried away, wave their newspapers from their firesides, as they shout to their wives and their little children, in front of their astounded servants, 'To Tunis, to Tunis.'

At once the men in power say to each other, 'You have to take account of public opinion.'

---

* France and Italy both had interests in Tunis. The Kroumirs, a tribe from the Tunisian side of the border, made forays into French Algeria which added to the existing dissension, whereupon the French moved in, ending by making Tunis a French Protectorate. Maupassant is writing just as these events were happening. A few months later he went for the first time to Algeria, for three months, to see for himself what was going on, sending regular despatches back to his newspaper *Le Gaulois*, some signed and some (the more controversial and anti-colonial ones) anonymous.

† Roustan was the French Minister in Tunis, suspected of a variety of corruptions, partly involving the Italian representative in Tunis, Maccio, with whom he was considered too friendly.

Then they arm, they move regiments about, they requisition ocean liners, they make the devil of a noise, with the secret thought, 'There will always be time to see what could happen.'

Whereupon the Bey of Tunis, who has other fish to fry apart from the Kroumirs, learns from the press that we are arming. He sends for the War Minister himself, and says to him, 'General, kindly take a decent army and go and see a little of what these good French are doing on our frontier.'

At once the Tunisian general leaves with at least five hundred men and, quite disconcerted, completely confused, goes in the direction of the French generals, who are no further on than he is. Then on both sides they wonder if they should attack each other or march together, land a few clouts or kiss. The matter is as clear as day.

*   *   *

Unless, however, the Government might not be feeling the ancient need of old governments: to have a war. When a drunkard has been some time without drinking, trying to reform, he can't last any longer and allows himself a little relapse. Oh, only a few glasses, just a little tipple. Isn't that it?

Governments make war like putting your fortune on 'double or quits'. Here however the stake is only small. Never mind, there will be reflected glory, it will add prestige, panache. War is an abyss that gives those at the top vertigo and, irresistibly, they go into it.

Though I myself will never forget a simple old Norman woman I saw one morning, who had stopped on the main road, with an immense umbrella and a huge basket in her hands, watching a company of infantrymen on manoeuvres in a field. As I was passing near her, she turned to me and said to me with a despairing, indignant, rebellious and lamentable air:

'There you are, monsieur, that's all they teach them! If it isn't a disgrace! They keep them from us five years for that, and they don't even have a trade when they come back. As if there wasn't enough poverty, don't you think, and illness, and everything, and you've got to let them kill lots of people, too!'

The little soldiers were marching forwards, backwards, all

raising their right feet in unison, then the left, turning their heads, marking time with an idiotic air and rigid eyes. The reverberating voice of their instructor rose into the morning air, and a lieutenant was walking about dejectedly, his hands behind his back.

On the road, a poor road mender went on with his lowly and monotonous task without respite. I said to the old lady, 'Yes, but my dear woman, they are learning how to defend their country too.'

She replied simply, 'You know, monsieur, we are worse than the animals.'

* * *

I would like everyone to have read the book published by the Belgian writer Camille Lemonnier, called *Les Charniers* (*The Charnel-houses*).

The day after Sedan, he left with a friend and visited on foot this killing area, this region of battlefields. He walked in human muck, slipped on spilled brains, wandered through rotting matter and infections for complete days and whole leagues. He picked up out of the blood and the mud 'those little dirty and disintegrating squares of paper, letters from friends, letters from mothers, letters from fiancées, letters from grandparents'.

Here, among a thousand others, is one of the things he saw:

The church at Givonne was full of wounded. On the threshold, mixed with blood, the straw crushed by feet was a fermenting heap.

Just at the moment we were going in, some infirmary orderlies, their grey aprons spotted with red patches, were sweeping through the entrance door a sort of foetid pool, like the one in a slaughter-house that the butcher's clogs stump about in.

... The hospital was in agony.... Some of the wounded were tied to their pallets with rope. When they moved, men would hold them by the shoulders to stop them changing position. Sometimes a pale face half rose up above the straw and watched, with tortured eyes, an operation on his neighbour.

You could hear some unfortunates shout and twist away when the surgeon came near, and they tried to stand up to run away.

Under the saw, they shouted more, an indescribable sound, hollow and raucous, as though flayed, 'No, I don't want to, no, leave me alone. . . .' It was the turn of a Zouave with both legs gone.

'Excuse me, everyone,' he said, 'they've taken my trousers off.'

He had kept his tunic, and his legs were bound up, towards the bottom, in rags from which blood was oozing.

The doctor began to undo these rags, but they were sticking to each other, and the last was applied to bare flesh. They poured hot water on this rough bandage and, as they were pouring the water, the surgeon removed the scraps.

'Who did you up like that, old man?' asked the surgeon.

'It was my pal Fifolet, Major. – Ouch, that's nearly pulling my hair. – He had the —— taken off, and me the legs. And I said to him, "Fifolet, here we are, done for." "Yes," he says to me . . . and then, bang! he falls flat on his face, head over heels, so I grab the greatcoat off a Prussian who was saying, "Aghrr, Aghrr!" as he scrabbled at his guts, and I wrapped my pal Fifolet in it as best I could. Then he got up and I just had time to shout "Well I'm damned. . . ." Then I go down, he grabs his tunic off and there it is on my legs, Major.'

The saw, long and thin, had drops on every one of its teeth.

There was a movement in the group. They put a stump on the ground.

'The second one to go, my brave fellow,' said the surgeon.

I put my head through a gap in the shoulders and I looked at the Zouave.

'Be quick, Major,' he said, 'I can feel that I'm going to go crackers.'

He was biting his moustache, white as death with his eyes starting out of his head. He was holding his leg with his own two hands, and shouting from time to time in a trembling voice an 'Oooh', which made you feel the saw in your own back.

'It's finished, my old dear,' said the surgeon as he took off the second stump.

'Goodnight,' said the Zouave. And he fainted.

I will leave poets free to celebrate this hideous mangling. I will let the politicians repeat 'War is sometimes inevitable. It has to be accepted. It is a dreadful necessity.' Yes indeed, I admit it. But do not go off on every occasion, like the Duke of Marlborough in the song, without knowing when and how you will return.

Without taking into account that after Tunis, the Kroumirs, etc., we will have to avenge the death of Colonel Flatters,* and that there no doubt we will come across other savages to chastise. So that Africa seems to be becoming a prolific seed bed, where wars will grow for us to order, which will allow its practitioners to keep their hand in and maintain the nation's feelings of magnanimity.

'La Guerre', *Le Gaulois*, 10 April 1881

---

* Colonel Flatters was on a mission in Algeria studying routes; he and his small escort were massacred in December 1880.

IN THE PRESENCE OF DEATH

Roses, roses, there are roses everywhere. The train is running between two endless fields of roses, and the wind blowing in your face through the carriage door seems like a whirlwind of perfumes.

Another smell, more penetrating, strikes you as well, as though it were floating over the first one and enveloping it; it is the powerful scent of the lemon and orange trees in flower, for above the fields of roses are terraces of dark leaves where golden oranges and yellow lemons are shining like stars, forgotten on the branches. Then the mountain rises up, all planted with these fragrant trees that carry their bright fruits and their exquisite flowers at the same time. An indolence comes over you in this abundance of scents, a desire to be overwhelmed by it, intoxicated even to exhaustion by these sweet exhalations.

The train is going on. To the right is the Mediterranean, motionless, dozing as well, deep blue; the caressing and careless sea which does not get tired, as other oceans do, with laborious tides against high cliffs. To the left is the wooded slope of the Alps, and, from time to time, through a gap in the mountains above the fields that make you constantly and involuntarily murmur with endless obsessiveness the banal and so often repeated phrase, 'Kennst du das Land, wo die Zitronen blühn', you sometimes see a snowy summit, still clothed in the harsh winter of the peaks.

Occasionally the train stops in a little town with a resonant name, and all along the barriers you see people watching the string of carriages. In spite of the sun and the heat they are wrapped in coats, leaning on a friend's arm, with miserable, profound, desperate eyes.

They are watching the train passing through and the new invalids who are getting off.

Because this warm and ravishing region is society's hospital and the cemetery of Europe.

* * *

Here we are at Menton. The Queen of England has left. The town is calm, left only to the dying. They drag themselves along, walking slowly, beside the peaceful waves and, when they lift their eyes, they can see the steeply sloping cemetery dominating the area like a citadel, at the top of a little hill.

In military towns fortresses are seen like that on the surrounding heights; in these towns of the dying, the impregnable position is made from tombs.

What a place it would be to live in, this garden where the dead sleep! Roses, roses, there are roses everywhere. They are blood red, or pale, or white, or veined with scarlet. The tombs, the paths, the places empty today and filled tomorrow, everything is covered with them. Their incredibly strong perfume is overwhelming, making head and legs unsteady.

All those who are lying there were sixteen, eighteen, twenty years old.

From tomb to tomb you go, reading the names of these creatures who were killed so young by incurable disease. It is a cemetery of children, like the white balls where married people are not allowed.

How it must be cursed in all the corners of the earth, this charming and dangerous land, death's pleasant and scented antechamber, where so many families, royal and humble, princely and bourgeois, have left someone behind, almost always a child, the object of their burgeoning hopes and their increasing affection.

From this cemetery the view extends on the left to Italy, as far as the headland where Bordighera stretches out its white houses to the sea, to the right as far as Cap Martin, which dips its leafy slopes into the water.

* * *

Everywhere along the length of this lovely coastline, we are in the presence of Death. But it is discreet, veiled, all good manners and modesty, well-brought-up, in fact. You will never see it face to face, even though it brushes by you all the time.

You could even say that people do not die in this area, for everything conspires with the fraud which this sovereign delights in, but how you can feel it, how you can catch its scent, how you can sometimes glimpse the end of its black robe! Certainly plenty of roses are needed and plenty of lemon blossom, so that you never catch in the breeze the frightful smell that drifts from the rooms of the departed.

There is never a coffin in the streets, never a funeral pall, never a tolling bell. Yesterday's thin walker no longer passes beneath your window, and that is all.

You wouldn't even know how these people disappear, if the one who used to be called 'La Camarde' sometimes didn't let you guess; it is as though she had let out a savage laugh to ridicule human fears.

She has some infernal tricks, some sinister jokes. All her appearances are burlesque and terrifying, full of devastating irony, of lugubrious and irresistible comedy. She is at home, she is enjoying herself.

In Paris hats are gravely removed as Death passes by. It goes about ceremoniously in dark vehicles highly ornamented with silver. Here it hides behind the doors.

Now in a big hotel where princes were staying, thin and dying princes, it was stated serenely that no one had passed away for a year. The air was so healthy, they said; the coast so full of health-giving pine trees, the sun so gentle, that even the most desperate cases were vying with each other to be cured.

126

People believed it; and when you no longer saw wandering about the gardens the gaunt face with glowing eyes of some walker with a frightful cough, you supposed he had gone back home, suddenly cured. Cured certainly, for ever and ever, and with no danger of relapse!

On the first floor was the son of a king, very ill but trusting, who was waiting for this health that was confidently promised him.

However, one night while everyone in the vast building was asleep, a terrifying noise suddenly shook it from top to bottom. First of all there was a resounding bang, like a thunderbolt; then a rumbling rolling similar to the reverberation of a thunderstorm, a horrifying din as if the fires in the heavens had burst through the roof of the building and flung all the beams and the tiles down the great staircase.

The Prince was upright in one bound and, his candle in his hand, opened his door, against which there had been a violent blow. He found himself face to face with a corpse lying beside the disembowelled coffin. The appalled undertaker's men were rushing down the stairs to get back their prey, which they had let fall from the top floor.

All the doors opened, all the condemned appeared, then stood aghast, motionless, drawn, before their companion of the day before, whose companion they would be obliged to be the day after!

In another hotel in the same town, a young woman – healthy and cheerful, that one – a visitor in this area that has as much pleasure as pain, accidentally went up a little concealed staircase. A manservant she met said to her, forgetting his place, 'Gracious, madame, are you coming up the stairs of the dead?'

* * *

Night is falling; a few villas are lighting up. People are dancing. The moon, low in the sky, casts motionless reflections on to the calm sea, and the ocean softly mirrors it, as though rubbed with light like the shimmering of moiré silk.

Beneath the orange groves the fireflies, those glowing insects, are dancing a strange ballet of flames in the scented air. They come, go, mingle, casting their intermittent and fantastic light, that quick light, no sooner lit than extinguished, which spangles the foliage with wandering stars.

How ravishing it is, this land of Death!

'Chez la mort', *Le Gaulois*, 8 May 1882

THE CARTHUSIAN
MONASTERY OF LA VERNE

Those who love the earth with that deep, tender and sensual love one has for people, sometimes go off for a month or two, alone, to some region which is very unknown, very wild, very new, and they go through it on foot, hour by hour savouring something like the happiness that must be felt at the possession of a virgin.

They are rare today, unexplored and deserted lands, especially if you don't want to leave France. Normandy is crossed by more walkers than the Boulevard des Italiens. Ancient Brittany hides a tourist, an unbearable tourist, behind every standing stone. The waters of the curative springs of Auvergne are taken by legions of sufferers who bring back bales of photographs taken on the domes, on the crags and on the precipices.

Where can you go? Yet in France there is a whole little region, very lonely and very beautiful, which is called the Maures mountains. Tomorrow a railway will go across it. Before it does, let us go to these unknown, uncultivated and uninhabited valleys, where soon perhaps as many villas will rise up as there are on the coasts of Cannes and Menton.

*　*　*

Where are they, these mountains? In the most well-known and most travelled-through part of France, between Hyères and Saint-Raphaël. Geographers teach us that in themselves they have a complete geological system. They have all the parts, all the classifications, all the components of their big sisters, the Alps and the Pyrenees.

Their flora is one of the richest in France. To the south the Mediterranean bathes their slopes, where one lovely beach follows another. To the north a fine river, the Argens, separates them from the rest of the world.

Six months ago, when the bathers from Saint-Raphaël walked over the long dune that goes around Fréjus Bay, after an hour's walk they would arrive at the edge of a wide waterway, whose sandy estuary would occasionally let you pass over with dry feet.

When you followed this river towards its source, you made your way in the middle of a sort of huge marsh, wooded and cultivated here and there. You would pass through groups of trees, through thick copses from which wild ducks, snipe, buzzards with big wings and clouds of wood pigeons would fly up at every moment.

Then, having realized that it was impossible to cross this wide sheet of water with its banks disappearing into reed beds, you would come back the same way, wondering what unknown region stretched out beyond it, and you would look, in the rosy haze of the setting sun, at the bluish mountains covered in pines, with their pointed and jagged summits rolling on out of sight towards the west.

Today a wooden bridge crosses the Argens. Here is the story of that bridge.

During the Second Empire a road was begun which was intended to join Saint-Tropez, situated at the far end of the Maures range, to Saint-Raphaël.

The road was built as far as the Argens. The Empire fell, the Republic was declared, and the works were stopped. There was nothing left to be done but to build the bridge over the river. They didn't build it.

130

So they had a wonderful ribbon of road for thirty-five to forty kilometres which was absolutely useless and perfectly maintained. No vehicle passed over that road which led nowhere, but the roadworkers laid stones, levelled it and swept it in order to use the funds put aside for the upkeep of a road that did exist.

That went on for twelve years. Then, since this state of affairs threatened to go on until the Empire was restored, about fifteen landowners in Grimaud Bay got together; each one gave a thousand francs and built an American-style wooden bridge.

So today you can get to the Maures mountains by land.

As soon as you go across the river you come to the site of a future town on the wooded slopes of the mountainside. The Mediterranean coast is covered with these planned towns. This one has something unusual about it. In the middle of a pretty pine wood which comes down to the sea, wide avenues open up in every direction. There is not a single house, nothing but the plan of the streets running through the trees. There are squares, crossroads, boulevards. Their names are even inscribed on metal plaques: Boulevard Ruysdael, Boulevard Rubens, Boulevard Van Dyck, Boulevard Claude Lorrain. One asks why all these artists? Ah! Why? It is because the development company said, like God himself before he lit up the sun, 'Let there be an artistic resort!' Bang! The development company! The rest of the world does not realize all that these words mean in terms of hopes, dangers, of money won and lost on the Mediterranean! The development company! That enigmatic, inevitable, significant, deceptive term!

However, the development company appears to be achieving its hopes in this spot for it already has buyers, and good ones, among artistic people. Here and there you read, 'Plot bought by Monsieur Carolus-Duran; Monsieur Clairin's plot; Mademoiselle Croizette's plot, etc., etc.' Yet... who knows? The Mediterranean companies are not in luck.

Nothing is more comic than this furious speculation which ends in spectacular bankruptcies. Anyone who has made ten thousand francs on a field spends ten million on land at twenty sous the square metre, to sell it on again at twenty francs a metre. The boulevards are marked, the water is brought, they make a start on the gas, and they wait for the buyers. The buyers don't come, but disaster does.

What is more, in this area, never say that it is cold, that it has rained, that the mistral blew. For the inhabitants would unite as an army to stone you to death. There is never frost, never water, never wind. Especially never wind! Because they really seem to believe that the mistral never blows, when it is blowing the stones off the main roads.

This winter a quite amusing anecdote was being told. The excellent landscape artist Guillemet, who during the summer does those remarkable views of Normandy which are well known, came to Saint-Raphaël. This painter (his friends are aware of it) has as much wit as talent. So one evening, when he was dining with important people from a development company, these men were praising the advantages of the area so energetically and with so much extravagance, that nothing else was talked about. One of them at last, one of the most important, said to the artist, 'Well, monsieur, have you done pretty pictures of our coast this winter?' Guillemet replied that he had worked as much as he could.

'Will you be doing one for the Salon?'

'Of course.'

'May we ask the subject?'

'Certainly. It is Saint-Raphaël in the snow.'

* * *

Let us go on with our journey.

The road follows the sea, winding along the coast through lovely countryside. To the right are the mountains, forty kilometres of peaks, of valleys where little torrents come down, a huge pine forest, without a village, without a house, almost without a road, a wooded desert.

But now we are arriving on the edge of a lovely bay which drops down in a gap in the mountains, Grimaud Bay. Opposite us, on the other coast, we can see a little town, Saint-Tropez, the home of the Bailli de Suffren.

Then we go through a village, Sainte-Maxime. In what far

outpost of the world are we then? You can read on the walls of this hamlet, which has only a few houses and which is traversed by two vehicles a day, 'By order of the Mayor, no trotting allowed in the streets.'

But they trot in the streets of Paris, Mr Mayor! And Paris is bigger than Sainte-Maxime, and there are a few more vehicles. They trot in Marseilles, Mr Mayor, and Marseilles too is bigger than Sainte-Maxime. Go on, let us trot, hang it all, we won't run over all your sixty inhabitants at once. But why, yes why, can't we go at a trot in the streets of Sainte-Maxime? Tell us the reason, please, because I can't see one.

Didn't I tell you that here we are at the end of the world! Though what a beautiful road all along the bay, with a big wooded mountain opposite and, at the end of the large basin, a pyramid of a village on a slope, dominated by the ruined tower of a château.

Here once more there are avenues in a superb pine forest. The development company has started a resort here. Indeed, it was right. I understand that the delightful painter Jeanniot owns land here.

At last you can make out a house, a beautiful old house looking over lovely countryside. It belongs to Monsieur de Raymond.

We are coming up to the village which winds up all round the hill. It is a former Moorish town. Here are their houses fronted with arches, with their narrow windows, the doors covered with beautiful wrought iron, the mysterious courtyards which are found in every Moorish house; on the terraced slopes grow tall palm trees, aloes with monstrous flowers, giant cactuses, all the plants of Africa.

The big summer sun is falling in sheets of flame on the little old city, strange and peaceful at the end of its bay. It is called Grimaud.

This is the birthplace of the ancient Grimaldi family.

We are following the Hyères road and we go through another village, Cogolin, then we turn right into a deep valley and we go into the uninhabited, the unknown.

No more road, just a rut that runs alongside a torrent and

constantly goes across it. You have to leap from stone to stone, at the risk of falling into holes full of water. Then nothing but pines and deserted valleys; always valleys, always pines; a vast, wild, bare country, with a calm and severe character, less turbulent than the region of big mountains, but more poetically beautiful, more expansively melancholy.

A small abandoned house could be seen in the distance, and this is what I was told.

About sixty years ago, two young people, a beautiful girl and a handsome youth, came and settled there, all alone. It was said on the quiet that it was a love story, an elopement. They lived together until last winter, happy, unbelievably happy, surrounded by their children. The man was eighty-two when his old companion discovered that he had a kept woman in the neighbourhood!

In one second all her happiness, her long happiness which was so lovely, fell apart, and the wretched woman jumped out of the window. She died the next day.

This simple and biblical drama is so admirably set in this austere countryside that it seems to have been invented by a poet. We are still going on and we are reaching a sort of impasse, in a big green amphitheatre surrounded with peaks. You have to climb up by a goat path; we go up, discovering all the time above the lower summits the whole of this region of wild ravines.

Then we pass between two peaks, go on along the mountainside, and soon a huge chestnut wood appears, clothing the mountain from top to bottom, and an enormous ruin, almost black, astonishing. A long line of arches against the rock are supporting on their vaults the ancient and crumbling abbey of La Verne.

Certain parts of it date from the ninth century. Today cows live in the cloister where the monks used to walk; a family of shepherds occupies a huge building, more recent, which seems to have been rebuilt in the seventeenth century.

This ruin, the most imposing one I know – the one that is best in the surroundings that are right for it, the one whose desolate face is most in accord with the sombre and imposing landscape – has the air of being the very soul of these mountains, of being the only inhabitant worthy of them, made for them.

We are still climbing up to the last peak, which needs an hour to scale, and nothing in the world is more beautiful than the view from up there.

Opposite, in the golden haze of the setting sun, the sea, the flat Mediterranean, gleaming, with the islands of Hyères which burst through its blue and motionless back like black specks. Around us a great wooded wilderness of valleys and ravines, the Maures mountains, and over there, to the north, the Alps, whose white summits can be seen shining here and there, like giant heads crowned with snow.

'Petits voyages', *Gil Blas*, 26 August 1884

CHRONOLOGY

1850   *5 August*, birth of Guy de Maupassant in the Château de
        Miromesnil near Dieppe, the residence of his parents (Laure
        and Gustave de Maupassant) from 1849 to 1853.

1856   Birth of Guy's younger brother Hervé in the Château
        d'Ymauville, Grainville-Ymauville (a dozen kilometres from
        the sea, described by Maupassant in *Une vie*), where the
        family lived from 1854 to 1859. Many holidays were spent
        with Maupassant's maternal grandmother, Mme Le
        Poittevin, at the nearby fishing port of Fécamp.

1858   The family spent the summer by the sea at Etretat and
        began buying land there, on which they built a house;
        Etretat, then a simple fishing village, was becoming a
        fashionable holiday resort.

1859   Guy went to school in Paris (Lycée Napoléon, now Henri
        IV) for the academic year 1859–60 only; it is not clear
        why he left. During this period the family left Ymauville
        to live in the house in Etretat.

1862   At the beginning of this year Guy's parents separated, his
        father living in Paris and his mother in Etretat with the
        two boys; apart from the one year of school above, Mme

de Maupassant had taught her sons herself and was well able to do so as she was an intelligent, cultivated and educated woman. The separation (they never divorced) seemed a reasonably amicable one, but Guy saw little of his father in his adolescence. He spent much of his free time with the local fishermen.

1863   In October Guy went as a boarder to the Institution Ecclésiastique in Yvetot, not far away, a Catholic religious foundation noted for its excellence in Classics; he did not enjoy the lack of freedom, sometimes feigning illness as a means of escape.

1864   He was saving for a boat – one like the local fishing boats.

1866   Guy left Yvetot, ostensibly due to a difference of opinion between his mother and the Superior concerning fasting in Lent. In April he went to the Lycée in Le Havre for two weeks only, then appears to have stayed at home, returning to Yvetot in October for the new school year. In spite of this disruption he still did well at school.

1868   In May he was expelled from Yvetot for expressing anti-religious sentiments. He was sent at once to the Lycée in Rouen, where he soon made contact with Louis Bouilhet, poet, dramatist, town librarian, friend of Maupassant's family and friend of Flaubert; Guy had been writing poetry for some years. At home in Etretat he met another poet, Algernon Charles Swinburne, who on 18 September had been dramatically rescued from drowning while staying with his friend George Powell; Guy had gone to the rescue but another fishing boat picked Swinburne up. Powell, a Welsh eccentric who had just bought a cottage in Etretat and was already known slightly to Guy, invited him to several bizarre lunches. Back at school in Rouen that winter, Guy saw Bouilhet regularly and sometimes Flaubert too, but he did not know Flaubert well at that stage.

1869   Bouilhet died unexpectedly, Guy passed the Baccalauréat examination soon after, and his school days were over. He registered for the first year of law in Paris.

1870   His law studies were interrupted by the outbreak of the Franco-Prussian War in July; he volunteered. Little is known of his movements during the war, though he was involved in the retreat of the French before the rapid Prussian advance on Rouen in December 1870. He was demobilized in late 1871; his father 'bought' a man to replace him, the only way to avoid serving a total of seven years in the army.

1872   Maupassant entered the Marine Ministry as a supernumerary. He achieved a permanent paid post in 1873, and stayed in the Ministry until 1878.

1873   He began to see a great deal of Flaubert, showing him his early attempts at writing, at first poetry, then prose. Their relations developed for seven years, at first a literary apprenticeship, then a close friendship. From 1872 on Maupassant's parallel activities on the river, with rowing-boats and girls, were pursued with vigour, intensity and enthusiasm. He always owned or part-owned a boat, sometimes several.

1875   He published his first story under a pseudonym in a provincial paper, and was also writing two plays (one an obscene comedy for private performance) and a story, 'Dr Heraclius Gloss' – none of them published in his lifetime.

1876   Finished another play and had some poems published, also two articles and a story. He had met many writers through Flaubert's Sunday afternoons – Zola, Turgenev, Alphonse Daudet, Edmond de Goncourt and the young Henry James. He began to see regularly what would later become the Médan group – Alexis, Céard, Hennique, Huysmans. By 1876 he also undoubtedly had syphilis, and from then on he had to live with very variable periods of illness or disability. The disease accompanied his literary career, like an increasingly intrusive shadow, to its end.

1878   Maupassant had been very unhappy at the Marine Ministry and, with Flaubert's help, managed to transfer to the Ministry responsible for Fine Arts and Education. Published two more stories and started his first novel, *Une vie*, but had to put it aside for a few years.

1879   His play *Histoire du vieux temps*, a one-act comedy, was performed successfully at the Théâtre Déjazet. Another story was published, he began writing 'Boule de suif' and had a poem published for which he was prosecuted for 'outrage to public morality'; the case was later dismissed thanks once more to Flaubert's help.

1880   A book of poems, *Des vers*, was published, which was well received, and 'Boule de suif' appeared in the collection *Les Soirées de Médan*, completely overshadowing the other stories by Alexis, Céard, Hennique, Huysmans and Zola. Maupassant had arrived. At the same time as his sudden fame came the death of Flaubert, who had become a kind of father figure to the younger man. Maupassant was now on his own and his life changed. He began to write for the newspaper *Le Gaulois*, took extended temporary leave from the Ministry (which became permanent eighteen months later), and the stories and articles began to pour out in an ever-increasing flood.

1881   He went to Algeria for three months for *Le Gaulois* and on his return also began to write for *Gil Blas*, as well as writing occasionally for other papers and magazines. He published his first collection of stories under the title of one of them, *La Maison Tellier*, a pattern which he followed through thirteen such collections.

1883   Maupassant now published his first novel, *Une vie*, had his own house, 'La Guillette', built in Etretat and, at the end of the year employed a valet, François Tassart, who remained with him to the end of his life.

1884   Published his first travel book, *Au soleil*, based partly on his time in Algeria for *Le Gaulois*. About this time he acquired a boat in the South of France, the *Louisette*, an old whale-boat.

1885   Published his second novel, *Bel-Ami*; he was thought to have produced unflattering portraits of actual journalists and newspaper proprietors, a charge he denied. He had ceased to write regularly for *Le Gaulois* before the publication of the book, but continued with *Gil Blas*.

1886   Published his third novel, *Mont-Oriol*. Set in the Auvergne, it is a rather bitter love story involved with capitalist speculation in the creation of a new spa, and with a comic and highly cynical view of medicine. In October Maupassant bought an 11-metre, 9.5-tonneaux racing cruiser, the *Audacieux* (previously *Flamberge*), renaming her *Bel-Ami*. He had the height of the mast reduced; he was not interested in racing, and that winter and the following spring he went on many short cruises.

1888   His fourth novel, *Pierre et Jean*, appeared together with his study on the novel, *Le Roman*. The novel was first serialized (late 1887), and *Le Roman* was first published separately in *Le Figaro*; this led to a lawsuit, as the newspaper made cuts which rendered part of the essay nonsensical. *Sur l'eau* appeared, and the short stories continued, but their pace was slowing.

1889   In January Maupassant bought a bigger boat, the *Zingara* (14.6 metres, with more accommodation), the second *Bel-Ami*; he sold the first one in June. Publication of his fifth novel, *Fort comme la mort*, which dealt with the society he now moved in and finely analysed the process of ageing. Maupassant's brother Hervé died, insane, in November, at the age of 33. One can see now that he must have died of syphilis, but the link between that form of insanity and syphilis was then only beginning to be suspected. Hervé's widow and small daughter were now dependent on Maupassant, who found himself very stretched financially.

1890   Publication of *La Vie errante*, his third travel book, based partly on a voyage in the *Bel-Ami* the previous autumn and on other journeys to Italy and North Africa; publication of his last collection of stories, *L'Inutile Beauté*. Maupassant's last novel, *Notre Cœur*, was also published this year, dealing with the impossibility of love in Parisian high society. He started two further novels, neither of which he was able to finish, and planned articles which were never written. He published nothing new after 1890.

1891   Maupassant now had very serious health worries. The physical problems worsened and, increasingly, he had mental difficulties as well. He moved despairingly from place to place consulting innumerable doctors.

1892 *1 January*, in Cannes, he made a failed suicide attempt; it was no longer possible to conceal the fact that he had General Paralysis of the Insane (one of the manifestations of the third stage of syphilis) and he was transferred to a clinic in Paris, becoming more and more demented.

1893 He died on *6 July*, a month before his forty-third birthday.

SELECT BIBLIOGRAPHY

Delaisement, Gérard, 'La composition des "Carnets de voyage" de Guy de Maupassant', *Revue des sciences humaines*, 92, 1958, 531–54

Franklin-Grout, unpublished memoirs, *Heures d'autrefois*, personal communication from Professor Jean Bruneau

Maupassant, Guy de, *Chroniques*, Paris, UGE, 10/18, 1980. This edition is not complete; 'Chez la mort', 'Bazaine' and 'L'Orient' were not included (Bibliothèque Nationale, Paris, microfilm D.97). The article 'La Guerre' of 1881 can be found as an appendix in *Lettres d'Afrique*, La Boîte à Documents, Paris, 1990

—— *Contes et nouvelles*, Paris, La Pléiade, Gallimard, 1974, 1979

—— *Les Lettres et les arts*, Paris, February, March and April 1888

—— *Sur l'eau*, Paris, Marpon et Flammarion, 1888; Folio, Gallimard, 1993

Muterse, Maurice, 'Souvenirs inédits de Maurice Muterse', *L'Angelus, Bulletin de l'Association des amis de Guy de Maupassant*, 5, 1994

Worth, G. J., 'Maupassant in England', doctoral thesis, University of Illinois, USA, 1954